I Remember

JOE DiMAGGIO

I Remember

JOE DIMAGGIO

*Personal Memories of the Yankee Clipper by the
People Who Knew Him Best*

David Cataneo

Cumberland House
Nashville, Tennessee

Published by Cumberland House Publishing, Inc., 431 Harding Industrial Drive, Nashville, TN 37211

Cover design by Gore Studio, Inc.
Text design by Mike Towle

Library of Congress Cataloging-in-Publication Data is available.
ISBN: 1-58182-152-2

Printed in the United States of America
1 2 3 4 5 6 7 8 9—06 05 04 03 02 01

CONTENTS

Acknowledgments   *ix*

Introduction   *xi*

1 **THE WAY HE WORE HIS HAT**   **1**

2 **BASEBALL'S FAMOUS STREAK**   **29**

3 **THE GREAT DIMAGGIO**   **51**

4 **HIS WAY**   **97**

5 **HARPO SPEAKS**   **155**

6 **THE LEGEND**   **185**

Notes   *215*

Index   *219*

About the Author   *224*

For My Dad, who taught me baseball

ACKNOWLEDGMENTS

Thank you to all who took the time to reminisce about Joe DiMaggio:

Dominic DiMaggio, Tommy Henrich, Bobby Brown, Jerry Coleman, Gil McDougald, Chuck Stevens, Doug Lyons, Jeff Lyons, Boo Ferriss, Johnny Pesky, Bobby Doerr, Matt Batts, Mel Parnell, Jack Lang, Red Auerbach, Dario Lodigiani, Everett Parker, John McNamara, Eddie Joost, Charlie Silvera, Bill Raimondi, Ron Croce, Tommy Holmes, Vernon Feen, Danny Onisko, George Kimball, Stephen Harris, Patricia Donnelly Harris, Al Gionfriddo, Sam Suplizio, Eddie Corsetti, Diane Cameron, Jim Hubley, Gus Zernial, Emil Mailho, Louis Almada, Lee Stine, Ed Lynch, Lee MacPhail, Jimmy Rego, Betty Glick, Joe Vetrano Jr., Steve Barath, Johnny Sturm, Bernie Esser, and Dino Restelli.

Special thanks to my old *Herald* colleagues, Crystal Hubbard and Joe Giuliotti; to Tim Wiles of the National Baseball Hall of Fame; to Bill Lenharth; to Jerry Horowitz; to Jim Gallagher; to P. D. Lighte; to

Andy MacPhail; and to Dick Beverage and his staff at the Association of Professional Ballplayers of America.

And thank you to Mike Towle and Ron Pitkin for their skill and patience.

INTRODUCTION

I was thirteen years old, and my best buddy and I had weaseled our way into the Americana Hotel in Manhattan to circulate among the dignitaries at the annual New York Baseball Writers Association of America dinner. We were two exuberant flies in the punch bowl, pestering many of the all-time greats: Stan Musial, Casey Stengel, Yogi Berra, Frankie Frisch, Charlie Gehringer, Whitey Ford, Billy Martin.

We could not, however, get into the bar, where other Hall of Famers hid. We waited outside the entrance behind a velvet rope line. We peered in at the tuxedoed men who milled about in the sepia tavern light, amid the cigarette smoke and tinkling ice in highball glasses.

We heard he was in there. Then we caught a glimpse of him, a tall, silver-haired gentleman, the guy we really wanted, the biggest autograph of them all.

"Geez," I said to my pal. "Joe DiMaggio."

"Well, to come out of there," my pal noted, "he's got to walk past us right here."

We waited. We made one of those young boy vows that we would wait forever, or longer. Nothing could make us move. Not Willie Mays, who passed by twenty feet away—to chase him would have meant abandoning our stakeout and perhaps missing Joe D. Not hotel security, which asked us please to take a hike.

Tom Seaver emerged from the bar, and we got him to sign our memo pads, all the while looking over his shoulder to make sure Joe D. didn't slip past. We would have ditched Tom Terrific in a minute if we had to.

Then, suddenly, he was striding out of the tavern light, into the bright hallway light, right there on the other side of the velvet rope, regal and legendary and wearing a jaunty smile, as if he had been truly enjoying himself with the boys in the bar.

"Mr. DiMaggio!" we screeched. Our voices crackled with despair and galloping adolescence. "Can we please have your autograph please?"

We must have sounded like violins way out of tune, playing a song he had heard a trillion times.

Joe DiMaggio stopped in his tracks. For a millisecond he stared down at the plush carpet and seemed to gather himself. The smile turned into a small, irritated smirk.

Uh-oh, I thought.

I did not want Joe DiMaggio to be cruel and annoyed with us. I knew if that happened, the whole magnificent night would be ruined, for the rest of time.

I knew a lot of stuff would be ruined. A huge chunk of the Yankee mystique—which consumed 90 percent of my waking hours in those days—would be spoiled. And then there were the goose bumps. How could I ever again get goose bumps—the kind you get during the Marseillaise scene in *Casablanca*—the next time he was introduced during Old Timers Day at Yankee Stadium? I deeply enjoyed those ovations, which seemed to rise from the past, from a great and grand time in baseball, in New York, in America.

And if Joe DiMaggio acted like an angry jerk, how could I ever break it to my father? He had told me all about Joe D., in the tone of voice that coal miners use when they tell their sons about Franklin Roosevelt.

My heart beat so loudly, I was afraid Joe DiMaggio would hear it.

He took my pad and pen—I recall the sensation of having to hand them up to him. He tapped the pen on the paper—perhaps a little harder than necessary—and sighed. He signed his name in big, neat loops.

"Thank you," I said.

"Okay," said Joe DiMaggio.

And everything was okay again—my memories, my father's memories, the goose bumps on Old Timers Days. Everything.

The point is, more than Willie Mays, more than Stan Musial, more than Yogi Berra, more than the president of the United States, more than an astronaut, more than the principal of my elementary school, what Joe DiMaggio did or thought really mattered to me. He was different.

I knew that for sure, but I was never really quite sure why. A few years later, I used my first paycheck to purchase the *Baseball Encyclopedia*, the good, thick book that lists the particulars of everybody who ever played major-league baseball. I looked up all the all-time greats, including DiMaggio, and the answer was not in the numbers. His statistics were terrific, but they didn't explain the goose bumps. As far as his career went, I was told, you really had to be there. I wasn't there.

I reached adulthood, got a job watching baseball games for a living as a newspaper reporter, and developed a healthy skepticism about ballplayers and heroes and myths. But the special feeling about DiMaggio did not go away. It survived and grew as I lived and learned and watched the twentieth century harden into some kind of context. I kept listening to people talk about him, and the feeling stuck that Joe DiMaggio was something special.

I never felt silly about it. I felt less silly when Joe DiMaggio died, and the newspapers were filled with memories of him. A lot of people got goose bumps over the Great DiMaggio, most of them people way more sophisticated than I was.

Which brings us to this book. I typed it, but it was really written by people who knew Joe DiMaggio, who played with Joe DiMaggio, who played against Joe DiMaggio, who watched Joe DiMaggio, who were touched by Joe DiMaggio. It was written by people who were there.

This book is not a biography. It is not a photograph of Joe DiMaggio—that's been done, most recently by Pulitzer Prize winner Richard Ben Cramer, whose critical study was published last year. This book is an impressionist painting of Joe DiMaggio. It helps explain the goose bumps.

—*David Cataneo*

I Remember

JOE DIMAGGIO

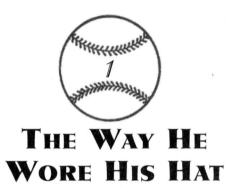

THE WAY HE
WORE HIS HAT

"He shaved with such distinction. It was beautiful to watch. Now it might be a little flaky to say that, but he was perfect in everything he did."

—PHIL RIZZUTO

There was something about him, something about how he went about his business, that tickled the poets, the truck drivers, the artists, the butchers, the ballplayers, the kings, and the kids who watched him. Joe DiMaggio collected fewer hits than Stuffy McInnis, fewer home runs than Dwight Evans, and a lower lifetime batting average than Fat Fothergill. But Joe DiMaggio's style made tough guys swoon.

"Baseball isn't statistics," Jimmy Breslin once observed. "It's Joe DiMaggio rounding second base."

Tell old-timers, people gray enough to remember Truman, that you never saw DiMaggio play and they'll say, "Well, you missed something." They say it grimly, as if they feel sorry for you.

What did you miss? Basically, a superb baseball player, so charming on the diamond that people just couldn't take their eyes off him. Pick a metaphor: He was Sinatra singing, Heifetz fiddling, Dietrich stepping out of a cab. Ted Williams claimed Joe DiMaggio was smooth, even while striking out. Branch Rickey declared that Joe DiMaggio was an artist. Casey Stengel simply said, "He made the rest of them look like plumbers."

When DiMaggio died, writers and other typists rounded up the usual adjectives: dignified, graceful, classy, effortless, elegant, regal. His pals and colleagues simply said Joe on the field and off the field always looked great. Toots Shor, saloonkeeper to the stars in New York's glory days, predicted that's what people would say someday when they filed past DiMaggio's open casket: "Joe, you look great."

Dario Lodigiani remembers the old neighborhood in San Francisco in the 1920s, and the nine DiMaggio kids at 2047 Taylor Street near Fisherman's Wharf. The second youngest was Joe, who liked to sleep late and did not like to fish. Joe showed huge hints of athletic greatness, with a little something extra:

I grew up with Joe. We went to school together. Francisco Junior High School. I lived on Telegraph Hill in North Beach, the Italian district. On the bottom of the hill is where Joe lived. And in between us was the playground. We were in that playground every day. And whatever sport was going on, we'd play it.

He was a quiet kid. Never said too much. But he was a good athlete, no matter what sport we played. We played baseball, we played touch football. Basketball. We even played tennis. He was a heckuva tennis player.

The way he ran. The way he carried himself. The way he walked around the ballpark. You could tell, there was a pretty good ballplayer. He looked like he was gliding. He was that kind of a ballplayer. His brother Dominic was the same way. They both played like they were floating.

Joe and I sold newspapers together. He sold newspapers on the corner of Market and Montgomery Street. He sold the *San Francisco Call-Bulletin*. If there was any vice he started in those days, he started smoking. I used to tell him, "What the heck are you smoking those cigarettes for?" He didn't know how to smoke them. He didn't inhale them. He was just burning them. He'd say, "It makes you look good."

⌒

DiMaggio believed in details. His hair was slicked just right. He was tall (six-foot-two) and slender (193 pounds), so clothes looked good on him. Baseball uniforms, even in the baggy flannel era, looked great on him.

The height of his stirrups was just so. The snappy angle of his cap was just so—too far back on the head, you look like a mechanic; too far down on the forehead, you look like a rube. He chewed gum (jaunty) instead of tobacco (sloppy). The jersey, of course, was always tucked in snug and neat, appearing tailored. "He never looked slouchy," said longtime Yankee colleague Tommy Henrich.

Infielder **Jerry Coleman** was his teammate with the Yankees for three seasons:

He showed up at the ballpark, shirt and tie, blue suit, every day. And he always knew who he was. And that's the important thing about DiMaggio. He always knew who he was and what he represented. He did everything just right.

He was one of the few players who had his pants lower than the rest. His pants were lower than most people long before it became the fad. His hat was cocked.

Nothing was an accident with him. It was all part of his image. This probably wasn't as true early in his career as it was later. Certainly after World War II, after he had created this image of the perfect person. He knew who he was.

The difference between Mantle and DiMaggio was very classic. Mickey never knew who he was. He never realized he was an icon, the greatest player in the country. Joe knew exactly who he was, what he was, and how to represent himself.

The Way He Wore His Hat

*DiMaggio knew what worked. He knew the power of poise
and dignity, with their awesome seductive qualities. He was
not movie-star handsome—some thought he photographed
downright homely—but he was immensely attractive
because he appeared sure of himself. He appeared calm.
He appeared unflappable.*

*He played a very difficult sport with splendid skill, and
he made it look easy.*

*"I think it was pretty obvious. Everything he did, he
did with finesse," said Dominic DiMaggio. "His natural
method of play was to just ease into a play and make it
look easy. And he did make it look easy."*

*That's what they all say. Joe DiMaggio made it look
easy. He seemed natural, fluid, never ungainly. It's a qual-
ity we adore in crooners, standup comics, actors, lovers,
and fighter pilots: Don't look like you're trying too hard.*

*When he was a young major leaguer, DiMaggio would
clomp into the dugout from the field and say, "How did I
look out there? Did I look okay?"*

*Legendary New York sportswriter Jimmy Cannon
described exactly how he looked out there. He wrote that
DiMaggio played with "unhurried grace" and "deft serenity."*
Jerry Coleman:

His presence, his posture, his demeanor on the field was
unlike any other athlete I've ever seen. He had an impe-
rial presence on the field that no athlete has ever had. I
don't care who you name, you could go to Michael
Jordan, you could go to Tiger Woods, nobody had his
presence on the playing field. His posture, his carriage.

5

He knew what to do and when to do it. He knew how to act. He was absolutely incredible.

~

Dario Lodigiani *played semipro ball around San Francisco with DiMaggio and was witness to a rarity— DiMaggio looking gawky and out of place on a baseball field:*

Joe was the shortstop on the team that year, and I was the second baseman. Joe never was much of a shortstop. He was one of those guys who would boot one and let a couple of runs in. And at bat, he'd knock in about six.

He broke into professional baseball as a shortstop. He was kind of erratic at shortstop. But when they put him in the outfield, boy, he became an outstanding player. I was playing with Oakland when Joe was with the Seals. I played against him in '35. You knew you were looking at a big-league ballplayer.

~

Louis Almada *also played against DiMaggio in the Pacific Coast League and also recalls a rarity: DiMaggio looking comical on the ball field:*

I started in 1929 in the Coast League, with Seattle. In '33, I was with the Missions.

Joe was very sensitive. I remember one time he was coming in on a fly. A lazy fly. He was coming in and he had his hands up. I don't know what happened. Maybe he stumbled or something. He had his hands up, and the ball hit him on top of his head. And it bounced up in the air and of course he caught it.

It was just an instant of something that never happened, happened. All the guys laughed. All the players laughed, and he resented that. It was the last out, and I was running out to center field. I went by him. I never even looked toward him. I kept running straight ahead. I didn't want to laugh.

He had rabbit ears. He heard the players laughing and yelling, "Get a basket out there!" and "You'd better put on a catcher's helmet!" Blah, blah, blah. Just popping off. He resented that. He was such a great fielder. He was very proud. Very much so.

Some players are cut out for the blue-collar job of catching, or the perky work at second base, or the duel-in-the-sun intensity of pitching. Joe DiMaggio was made for center field, or maybe center field was made for Joe DiMaggio.

*Yankees manager **Joe McCarthy** moved the rookie around the outfield as the kid recovered from leg and ankle injuries to start the 1936 season:*

Well, we knew he could play, so we just waited for him to get well. Ben Chapman was my center fielder then, and he was a pretty good one. He could really go get a fly ball. DiMaggio had never played center field. I watched him go back on a ball, and I knew he could play it. I started him in left field after his foot got better, and then I moved him over to right field for a while. I wanted to make sure he was comfortable before I put him in center field. Finally, I decided he was ready, so I moved him into center field. He never would have become the great outfielder he was if I hadn't moved him. He needed that room to roam in Yankee Stadium. That's the toughest center field in baseball and only the real great ones can play out there. That's a lot of ground for a man to cover.[1]

He swung the bat sweetly and ran the bases with skill, but DiMaggio's game was most beautiful in the field. That's where he brought out the Walt Whitman in people.

Cannon wrote that DiMaggio chased fly balls "concerned only with the defeat of awkwardness." Wilfrid Sheed wrote, "In dreams I can still see him gliding after fly balls as if he were skimming the surface of the moon."

Some say he was the best, some select other legends. Usually it comes down to a matter of taste. Entering the arena as DiMaggio limped off, Willie Mays turned out to be a more proficient center fielder, but never more pleasing than DiMaggio. Mays had style, too. He ran out from under his cap (he wore it a little big, so it would fly off) and chased fly balls as if jitterbugging. Beautiful. DiMaggio *chased fly balls as if he were waltzing. A different sort of beautiful.*

Tommy Henrich *describes DiMaggio's greatest catch, a long blast to left-center field by Detroit Tigers slugger Hank Greenberg in the summer of 1939:*

At the crack of the bat, he sees the ball take off and he's got a doggone good idea where that ball is going and where it's coming down. That's what Joe did. He turned around. He ran as fast as he could to the center-field fence and when he got within one full stride—that would be about seven or eight feet—over his left shoulder, he turned his head to the left, and there is the ball. And he got his glove up and caught the ball. And that is the first time he looked for that ball since the crack of the bat.

I call that the best one I ever saw. I'm telling you, DiMaggio was impressed by that, too. How do I know? Because he made the only mental error that I ever saw him make right after it. Do you know what he did? He started to run in with the ball and it was only the second out.

Earl Averill was on first base for the Tigers. He had rounded second when he saw DiMaggio catch the ball. He turns around. And DiMaggio is running in with the ball, slowly. It dawned on Joe that, holy geez, that isn't the third out. Averill got back to first base. Standing up.

So that was a mistake on Joe, right? That's the only one I ever saw.

Joe D. as a young outfielder for the Seals in 1935, known as much for his arm as his bat. (AP/Wide World Photos)

THE WAY HE WORE HIS HAT

Yankee right-hander **Spud Chandler** *threw the pitch to Greenberg and for the rest of his life remembered DiMaggio's catch as the greatest he ever saw:*

It was probably the greatest play a lot of people ever saw. It's hard to believe that a fellow could hit a ball as high and as far as Greenberg did and have it caught. It was hit all the way to what we used to call the graveyard out there in center field by those monuments. About 460 feet.

That occurred late in the season in 1939. We were way behind in the game at the time, and there was nothing at stake. But that's the way Joe played ball—everything was at stake for him, all the time.[2]

⌒

Other players watched, admired, learned. In the early forties, **Tommy Holmes** *was a Yankee center-field prospect, a job without much room for advancement. He later prospered with the Boston Braves.*

Holmes remembers a few spring afternoons in the outfield with Joe D.:

I signed with the Yankees in '41. I went to spring training with them. He was the class, without a doubt. As a player, to the other players, he was attractive. Even in the batting practice, he got a beautiful swing. He wasn't the fastest, but he had a beautiful gait. When we played some games, I was in left field. In the outfield, Joe used to glide. Joe didn't dig into the ground. He was smooth as silk. And you copied. You always copied from the best.

Because of him, I got chased out of town. I go down to spring training, I'm flying. I'm ready. So I'm in center field and I'm running around, and Joe McCarthy says, "Gee kid, you got a good arm." I said, "Why don't you put me in center, put Joe in left field, and Keller in right?" You can guess what he said to me. Later on, they optioned me back to Newark.

*DiMaggio's allure reached into the stands, from the box seats to the upper deck. **Everett Parker** was a teenager growing up in Brooklyn and rooting desperately for the New York Giants in the late thirties. Still, he paid a few visits to the Bronx to see New York's American League entry. Joe DiMaggio caught his eye:*

He was as smooth as could be. He used just a minimum of effort to do what he had to do. A ball would be hit to the alleys, and they had deep alleys at Yankee Stadium. You'd say, "Oh, my God, that's two or three bases." And you'd be happy if you were an anti-Yankee fan, like I was. But DiMaggio would be there. He'd just move on the ball beautifully. He didn't catch it over his shoulder. He caught it even easier. He never seemed to have to dive. He never seemed to have to roll.

I used to think, *Geez, why didn't I grow up rooting for these guys? Why am I rooting for the Giants?* Rooting for the Yankees, with DiMaggio leading them, was like rooting for General Motors. That's how it always seemed to be. You knew they were going to grind you out.

You can't teach it, what he could do. When Willie Mays came along, he was flamboyant. He got the job done with a lot of flash. He was also a great player, with an altogether different style. DiMaggio was professional. Smooth.

Of all the guys I've seen, the best would have to be DiMaggio. Williams and Mays right up there. Musial was something else. But DiMaggio was the best, even over Willie Mays. I'd have to give it to DiMaggio. Williams was the best hitter. Mays was the best fielder. But when you put it together, I'd give it to Joe D. It hurts to say that, because I'm a Giants fan.

Ernie Sisto was a news photographer for the New York Times:

I can still see DiMaggio out there in center field. I saw him play so many games, almost every game he played in New York.

When he was out there in center field, it was like a song, he had that graceful rhythm. A guy would hit a ball. He'd take a look at it and then he'd turn away and he'd run to a certain spot. Then he'd turn around and be ready. He knew where that ball was gonna go before the ball got there. He made it look so easy. It was uncanny, the naturalness.

I can still see him running out to his position. He used to step on second base all the time when he went out to the field and when he came back into the dugout. But he had another little thing. It wasn't a superstition, but every time he went out to center field to play his position he'd spread his legs far apart and then pull down on the visor of his cap, sort of getting himself all set. He did it every time. I still see that picture of him out there.[3]

Sam Suplizio was a high school kid growing up in western Pennsylvania. In the summer of 1946, he convinced his father to drive him to New York City:

I was a center fielder all my life. You know how young kids play shortstop, second base, outfield, everywhere? I never played anywhere but center field. I was a center fielder. I was going to New York to see Joe DiMaggio. Period.

I remember the game well. He looked like he must have been twenty feet tall. You know what impresses you? He ran a ball down. They hit a ball to left-center field. There were no monuments there then. The wall in center field was way deep. It's where the monuments are now. You could run forever in left center. He ran a ball down, just graceful, like there was just nothing to it. Long strides. He took it over his left shoulder like it was just nothing.

THE WAY HE WORE HIS HAT

I turned to my father and said, "My, God."
And he threw somebody out at third base, too.

⌒

Ossie Vitt managed the Cleveland Indians, 1938–40:

Everybody talks about Joe DiMaggio's hitting. But Joe
won more games with his glove and arm than with his
bat. When I was managing the Indians we were playing
the Yankees one day in that big Municipal Stadium in
Cleveland. We had the bases loaded and two out and
Hal Trosky, our first baseman, cow-tailed one out of
sight. I waved our runners around. "DiMaggio," I said,
"get that one!"

He did! He went back to the wall, over four hundred
feet away, and speared it one-handed. So okay, I figured,
DiMaggio can play deep. The next time up Trosky took
his usual toehold and DiMaggio was in deep center. But
Hal hit the ball on his fists for a blooper behind short.
"Okay," I muttered, "get that one, DiMaggio!" He did—
raced in and took it off his shoe tops. After that, I was
through challenging DiMaggio. I never did it again."[4]

⌒

*If center field was the perfect complement to DiMaggio's
style, so was New York.*

*He was no sophisticate when he arrived in the big city—
when a reporter asked for a quote, he thought the ink-stained*

15

wretch wanted a soft drink—but DiMaggio was smart enough to keep his mouth shut, keep his eyes and ears open, and learn. And somewhere inside him there was enough passion to like the place, its intensity and its offerings, and to appreciate what E. B. White called its "massive doses of supplementary vitamin—its sense of belonging to something unique, cosmopolitan, mighty, and unparalleled."

*Boyhood chum **Dario Lodigiani** remembers the big-city effect on the kid from down the hill:*

When we were kids, he dressed clean, just like anybody else, in whatever our parents could afford to get for us. Joe was a kid like any other kid.

But before he left for New York, Lefty O'Doul was his last manager with the Seals. O'Doul was New York–smart from all the years that he played in the major leagues. He played with New York, especially. He kind of smartened Joe up, told him what to do, what to wear, how to dress.

First thing you know, when he comes back, when you see him, Joe looked like a department store. He looked great. He always looked great.

⁓

DiMaggio was lucky to land in New York and lucky to land on the Yankees. (Of course, the Yankees were lucky to have DiMaggio, too.) They were perfectly suited to each other and brought out the best in each other. They were a great match that over the years turned perfect. Imagine Joe DiMaggio on a team nicknamed the Gashouse Gang (Saint

Louis Cardinals), or on a team nicknamed Dem Bums (Brooklyn Dodgers). Imagine him on a team that wore uniforms featuring a cute bear toting a bat (the Cubs) instead of a team that wore midnight-blue pinstripes.

To understand Joe D.'s style, you must understand the style of the McCarthy-era Yankees. One became indistinguishable from the other.

Tommy Henrich remembers the Yankee way, which was DiMaggio's way:

The first time I walked into the Yankee clubhouse, on Opening Day 1937, I shook hands with all the guys. They were very cordial. They didn't overdo it. They shook hands and they went on their way. In short order, when I met all those fellows, I got this feeling. And I got it today. You're with a bunch of pros. That was evident. And as long as I was there with McCarthy, it stayed there the same way. The pride of the ballplayers. I'm not talking about the front office at all. The players and McCarthy.

DiMaggio's Yankees had a swagger. **Johnny Sturm** was first baseman on the '41 team:

I remember one time, we had Jimmie Foxx picked off first base. And I'm screaming at Dickey, "Throw the god——ball!" He never did throw the ball. At the end of the inning, I came on into the bench, and Dickey says, "John, don't worry about trying to pick anybody

17

off. We'll be seven runs ahead of them by the fifth inning." That's the kind of ball club we had at that time.

⁓

*Third baseman **Bobby Brown** was DiMaggio's teammate, 1946–51:*

I think the standards were set before Joe got there. He fit in. All those old Yankees, like Tommy Henrich and Rizzuto and Charlie Keller and DiMaggio, you watched those guys and they all comported themselves in the same manner and they all dressed correctly. They just acted the way a world's champion should act. The older Yankees passed that on to the younger ones.

I met Joe in 1946 when I went to spring training. I think when you saw Joe in that Yankee uniform, and you were wearing the same uniform, you knew you were in the big leagues. There wasn't any question of where you were. He had that air about him. That he was *the* player.

⁓

Jerry Coleman:

During his heyday, the Yankees dominated the sports world like no other team ever. And consequently, he lived that image.

He was that image. And he really was *the* Yankee. That had something to do with the way he carried himself. I don't know if he would have felt so good if he was with the Saint Louis Browns.

~

*Legendary basketball coach **Red Auerbach**, who built a classy hoop dynasty with the Boston Celtics, remembers where he got the idea of how winners should carry themselves:*

Joe and I were talking one day. I was talking to him about the dress code. I talked to Joe McCarthy about it, too. DiMaggio said, "You know, when you dress like a champion, you feel like a champion. If you act like a champion, you're more apt to be a champion." Rather than a slob, you know?

I copied the Yankees' dress code over the years in Boston. You had to wear a jacket, shirt, and tie to the games. A guy like Joe DiMaggio actually looked and acted like a champion. If you could get a whole team to look and act the way DiMaggio did, you'd have a helluva club on your hands.

~

DiMaggio basked in a reputation for poise afield, which isn't easy for a baseball player. He was unflappable in the face of a game that makes everybody flap. Baseball schemes to mortify you a thousand times a minute. The baseball diamond, in front of tens of thousands of fans, is

19

not the ideal workplace for someone who treasures dignity. As far as humiliating endeavors go, baseball is in the same league as dating and child rearing.

Even Little Leaguers know it. There is no routine sports failure more embarrassing than striking out—the wild flailing and missing, the catcher chortling and tossing the ball to third, the long return walk to the dugout, bat in hand.

DiMaggio simply avoided it. In the summer of '41, for instance, when he batted .357 with thirty home runs, he struck out thirteen times. (For comparison, in 1956, the year he won the Triple Crown, Mantle struck out ninety-nine times.)

Red Sox right-hander **Boo Ferriss** faced DiMaggio from 1946 through 1948:

DiMaggio had that wide stance at the plate. You couldn't throw him anything slow or change speeds on him. He didn't overstride. He didn't stride very much. He always got a piece of that ball. You didn't fool him too much.

He was easy on the eyes when he batted. He was not jittery, or curled into a corkscrew, or prone to odd leg kicks. He favored long, heavy bats with thin handles. He stood nearly straight up in the box. His feet were planted wide apart. The bat was cocked behind his ear. When he swung, he had no hitch, took no giant step—he barely lifted his front spike from the dirt.

THE WAY HE WORE HIS HAT

Chuck Stevens *played first base for the Saint Louis Browns in 1946 and 1948:*

DiMaggio and Williams, they were the only two I have ever seen this happen to. When they went into the batting cage to take batting practice, all activity stopped. The opposing players stopped anything they were doing to watch it. And half of his teammates did, too—of course, it was old hat to them.

The ballpark was quiet. And all you could hear was wood on the ball. Players are as big a fan as anyone in the world. They knew they were looking at something special.

~

On the baseball field, Joe DiMaggio was cool. He was like a Hemingway character, without all the animal killing and drinking. He was calm, stoic, unreadable in an age when that sort of thing was admired. He did not have the joy of Willie Mays, who came right out and said he liked to "play happy," or the mania of Ted Williams, who spit at fans, swore generously, and hurled bats. He was Gary Cooper in flannel.

Once, DiMaggio was asked why he didn't let his hair down and throw a base or a tantrum now and then, and he said, "I can't. It wouldn't look right."

Chuck Stevens *remembers DiMaggio always under control, always looking right:*

There was a great deal special about him, because he did everything with finality. He beat you fielding; he beat you running; he would beat you throwing; he would beat you with the bat. But he never, ever showed any emotion.

He went all out without making a big to-do about it. One of the guys that I always admired, and I'm not saying this in a derogatory way, because he's a very dear friend, was Enos Slaughter. Enos Slaughter went all out. But he made a lot of noise about it. He whooped it up all the time. He was very vocal. Joe did all the things that Slaughter did, but he did it quietly and, bottom line, a little better.

Bobby Brown:

You never could tell what Joe was thinking. He was the same whether he hit a home run or whether he popped up. Nothing changed. He didn't have an expression on his face of great dismay, nor would he have an expression on his face that he was exulting.

If he hit a home run, he didn't run around the bases clenching his fist and jumping in the air. And if he popped up, he had the same gait. He was the same every inning of every game.

DiMaggio was easy to count on, because he was hard to rattle. In the rough-and-tumble thirties and forties, pitchers worked to rattle you.

*Every competent pitcher attempted to unnerve
opposing hitters by throwing close to them and even
sometimes by plunking them. Pitchers tried to make batters sweat, and DiMaggio tried to never let anybody see
him sweat.*

Bill Raimondi *was a catcher with the Oakland Oaks
and played against the young DiMaggio in the Pacific
Coast League:*

In 1933, he was with San Francisco, and I came to the
Oakland club. We played against each other for about
three years. I thought he was the best ballplayer I had
ever seen. He could do everything—he could run, he
could hit, he could throw, he could field. He was a very
quiet guy on the field. Didn't bother anybody. He'd
hardly say hello to you.

I was a catcher. Nothing fooled him. He ripped
everything. In the Coast League, they'd knock you
down. He'd just move out of the way. Never said a word.
Go back up there and take his cuts.

It was his first year or second year. He had trouble
with one of our pitchers. I think it was Roy Joiner. He
came close and Joe took exception. They had a little
skirmish. No blows were struck. They just started talking to each other. I don't know what he said, but I could
imagine it was a swear word or two.

That was the first time I ever saw Joe get riled up.
That was probably the only time.

There was one person DiMaggio often lost his temper with, but seldom showed it.
   Bobby Doerr:

I saw him mad once. It was running the bases. He was very seldom thrown out on the bases, but this day he made a mistake, and I could hear him swearing at himself.[5]

———

DiMaggio cultivated a look of comfort on the ball field. Pitchers hated batters who looked comfortable. In Game 5 of the 1941 World Series, Brooklyn Dodger hurler Whitlow Wyatt thought DiMaggio was digging in a little too deep—planting his feet firmly in the batter's box—and brushed him back twice in one at-bat.
   Tommy Henrich *remembers a rare growl from the cool, calm, silent DiMaggio:*

It was the last game. Whitlow Wyatt did not knock Joe down, but I think the feeling was that he was coming mighty close on a few pitches.

Joe Gordon drove in a couple of runs and I hit a home run. I don't think this incident happened right after I hit the home run. Anyway, DiMaggio made the second out of an inning. He's crossing from first base, where he had rounded it. It was a fly ball. Deep, but not too well hit. He's crossing from first base through the pitcher's mound to our dugout. And as he went by—I saw him do this—you could see him saying a few words as he passed Whitlow.

And as he went past him, Whitlow looked like he was going after Joe, too. "C'mere, you son of a gun." I don't know if they wanted to talk it over, or what. But they were both intense, no doubt about that. Of all things, Mickey Owen ran right out to the mound just so something would not start. They broke it up in a hurry. That was the end of it. Nothing ever happened.

It sure was out of character for Joe. He wasn't one to make a big show out of it.

~

Henrich remembers DiMaggio's going to great lengths to stay in character:

This was Tex Hughson, in Boston. McCarthy is managing Boston. This was one of the few mistakes, when it comes to psychology and baseball players, that I can ever recall McCarthy making.

Tex Hughson absolutely drills Joe. In the midsection. In the stomach. And head-on. You know that's got to burn, boy. A fastball, right there. It didn't hit any ribs. The ball fell down.

DiMaggio, just like that, turned to his left and threw his bat, not hard, but just in a gesture of disgust.

McCarthy, with the Red Sox over there, said, "Watch him. He won't even rub." That's what he said.

I Remember Joe DiMaggio

It was supposed to build up the Red Sox to try to be as tough as DiMaggio.

And he didn't rub. And he did not run to first base. He walked. So you know he's hurting. You just think about it. He never walked to first base in his life.

⌒

*He was so cool, his tiniest lapses were remembered for decades. **Jerry Coleman** can still see DiMaggio, miffed, letting down his guard for a moment:*

Something happened on the field that didn't appeal to him. He came into the dugout and kicked the ball bag. He thought it was an empty bag. It turned out to be a bag of balls. It was obvious that he had hurt his toe.

We all looked the other way. You didn't want to go, "Hee-hee-hee, look what happened to Joe." If it had been somebody else? We probably would have. But DiMaggio was different.

⌒

It was the sixth game of the 1947 World Series, bottom of the sixth, Brooklyn leading by 8-5. The Yankees had runners on first and second and DiMaggio stepped up.

DiMaggio crushed a long drive to deep left center and everyone in the ballpark thought the game was tied on a heroic homer by Joltin' Joe.

The Way He Wore His Hat

Al Gionfriddo was playing left field for the Dodgers at that moment:

I was fortunate to be in the right place at the right time. I was with Pittsburgh earlier that season, and I was traded to the Dodgers. And I could run. So fate played a role in it.

I'm playing pretty close to the line. I figured that was where they were going to pitch him. In case he pulls the ball, you don't want two runs to score.

When he hits the ball, he hits it into left-center field, where the bullpen is. I just put my head down and ran, looked toward home plate once, and kept on running as I'm looking over my shoulder. When I looked over my shoulder the second time, I was very near the bullpen gate. I jumped and I caught it—I'm left-handed—over my left shoulder with my back toward home plate as the ball was going over the fence. The wall was very low where the bullpen gate was. It would have been out if I hadn't caught it. When I came down, I turned and hit my butt against the bullpen gate. When I came down, I just looked in my glove to make sure I had it.

⌒

When DiMaggio saw the ball caught, and caught not too gracefully, he looked down at the baseline and flicked his right shoe at the dirt. It was a small, aw-shucks display, but for DiMaggio it was an outburst.

I Remember Joe DiMaggio

Gionfriddo:

Afterward they showed pictures in the paper and talked about how this was the first time Joe ever reacted.

We hit the banquet circuit together. I don't know how many places we went. And we stood up there together and Joe said, joking, "Look at this guy, compared to me." I'm five-foot-six. But he praised me more than anything else.

(Gionfriddo's glove, the one he used to catch the ball that made Joe D., the Hemingway character, kick the dirt, is in the Hall of Fame.)

BASEBALL'S FAMOUS STREAK

"Born the year of DiMaggio's streak."
>—PETE ROSE, when asked his age

From May 15 until July 17, 1941, America was obsessed with Joe DiMaggio. He was getting a hit every day. The Germans were in Paris, the Japanese were in China, and the United States was hoping to skip it this time. And DiMaggio gave everybody something else to think about for a while.

DiMaggio was in a hitting streak—batting safely in each game—and Americans went about their summer afternoons in homes, factories, offices, and shops, in cabs, on buses and trolleys, on sidewalks and front stoops, in barns and pool halls, calling out and wondering if DiMag had gotten another one. He was the topic of conversation. He was a game show, a soap opera, a murder trial, an election recount, and a giant daily lottery all rolled into one.

The Streak picked up DiMaggio and dropped him a few steps higher on the ziggurat, promoting him from sports hero to folk hero, taking him out of Ty Cobb's league and putting him up near Babe Ruth, just short of Paul Bunyan.

In the middle of the Streak, a summer high school history class in Cincinnati was polled to name the greatest Americans of all-time. Abraham Lincoln was third, George Washington was second. DiMaggio was first.

It was an amazing achievement. During the Streak, DiMaggio hit fifteen home runs, four triples, and sixteen doubles, drove in fifty-five runs, scored fifty-six, and batted .408 (91-for-223). He struck out only five times.

The Streak inspired bandleader Les Brown to write a No. 1 hit about "Joltin' Joe DiMaggio." And when novelist Raymond Chandler sat down to write the screen version of his *Farewell, My Lovely*, he had hard-boiled detective Philip Marlowe follow the Streak and wonder, "Would he hit safely in every game forever? It seemed that way. And why not? He was only twenty-six and playing baseball in the sunshine. He heard little boys cheer, not cry."

Big boys were cheering about it for the rest of the century.

"You can talk all you want about (Rogers) Hornsby's .424 average and Hack Wilson's 190 RBIs," Ted Williams said in his old age. "But when DiMaggio hit in those fifty-six consecutive games, he put a line in the record book. It's one that will never be changed."[1]

Even DiMaggio was impressed. He knew the Streak's place in history.

When he was dying, the eighty-four-year-old legend was in a Florida hospital, in intensive care, hooked to tubes as lung cancer whittled at him.

His old barber and buddy, Angelo Sapio, visited and made the kind of small talk people make when in the presence of someone gravely ill. Sapio mentioned that he had recently run into a guy who claimed he was at the game in Cleveland in 1941 when DiMaggio's famous fifty-eight-game hitting streak ended.

Struggling to talk, DiMaggio tugged at Sapio's sleeve and pulled him down close to the bed.

"It's fifty-six," the dying DiMaggio whispered.[2]

He had a history. In the summer of 1933, DiMaggio was eighteen years old and playing for the San Francisco Seals in the highly regarded Pacific Coast League. From May 28 through July 25, he got a hit in sixty-one straight games, shattering the PCL record of forty-nine.

Dario Lodigiani, *DiMaggio's younger chum from the old neighborhood, followed the Streak closely:*

There were people who would go to the ballpark, and when Joe got a hit, they'd leave. They just wanted to see Joe get his hit. I went out there as a kid a number of times to watch him.

A lot of the pitchers in the (Pacific) Coast League would say, "Well, when we play the Seals, I'll stop

31

him." There was a fellow named Buck Newsom, who played in the big leagues. He was pitching for Los Angeles. He came out and made a statement: "If when we play the Seals, he's still got that streak going, I'll stop him." The first pitch he threw to Joe, Joe hit it against the wall for a double.

There was another fellow who later pitched with the Cardinals and a number of clubs in the majors. He did the same thing. He said he was going to stop him, and Joe creamed the first one off of him.

⁓

Seals teammate **Lee Stine**:

The whole thing was spectacular to last that long. People were watching him every day after he got up around thirty-five or forty. They sure were. They had a pitcher in Los Angeles by the name of Bobo Newsom. We were playing in L.A. He got a couple of strikes on Joe. And he was a pretty chesty guy, Newsom. He knocked Joe down. So the next pitch, Joe hit it out over the center-field fence, which was about 410 feet. A line drive off of him. That just shows you he had a lot of guts. It didn't bother him at all. He was a great prospect. He could just do everything outstanding. He had all the ability in the world.

⁓

DiMaggio played only thirteen seasons and injuries forced him out of a number of games over the years, yet his exploits at the plate were truly extraordinary, starting with his fifty-six-game hitting streak in 1941. (AP/Wide World Photos)

I REMEMBER JOE DIMAGGIO

Charlie Silvera, *a future backup catcher with the Yankees, remembers being eight years old and counting DiMaggio's hits:*

I only lived eight blocks from Seals Stadium. I would go and my mother would take me, and I saw him when he was on that hit streak. I followed him all the way through. A lot of people did.

Eddie Joost, *who would go on to a solid major-league career, remembers the DiMaggio of that summer:*

I was playing for the Mission Reds in '33. I was only sixteen years old. I was playing third base one day in San Francisco at the old ballpark. He hit a ball right between my legs before I could get my glove down. That's how hard he could hit the ball.

Emil Mailho:

I played for the Oakland Oaks. I was an outfielder. When he was on that hitting streak, I caught the last out he made in the game that ended the Streak. People said to me, "Why the hell didn't you drop it?" I said, "They never drop them when I hit them."

One time during the Streak, they were playing against the Sacramento Solons. He hit a ball to deep short. The guy kind of missed it, booted it, and they gave him a hit on it to keep the Streak going. It was in the paper that they helped Joe with the Streak. You know, things were tough in the thirties. People paid money to come out and see Joe hit.

The Streak of '41 started after a small slump—DiMaggio was held hitless in back-to-back games by Cleveland Indians aces Bob Feller and Mel Harder. Then, in the first inning of a game against the White Sox, he singled.

*By that summer, **Dario Lodigiani** had joined his old schoolmate in the big leagues:*

I was with the White Sox. The first hit that Joe got to start his streak, I was playing in it. I was playing third base. He hit the ball off of Edgar Smith. He hit the ball between Luke Appling and myself. It was a ground ball through the infield.

By June 10, the Streak was up to twenty-four. DiMaggio was hitless in his first three at-bats against the White Sox when he stepped to the plate in the seventh inning.

He smashed a bullet to third baseman Lodigiani, who knocked down the hot shot, retrieved the ball, and barely missed throwing out DiMaggio at first base.

Yankees shortstop **Phil Rizzuto** *remembers:*

That was the way he was hitting in that streak. He always hit a ball well. Very seldom, if ever, would he hit a ball on the handle or on the end of the bat, like most of us "normal" ballplayers. Every time he hit it, it was almost always good wood. But now he was outdoing himself. Everything he hit was a bullet. I'll never forget Joe telling me once—and he's the only man that ever said it, the only man that could ever say it—that he could hit a ball with the third baseman playing deep and still handcuff him. In other words, if he hit a low line drive and that third baseman had his hands on his knees, the ball would be by him before he could actually get set to field it.[3]

Lodigiani:

He hit a coupla ground balls at me, and I knocked them down and threw him out. Then the last time up, he was 0-for-3 and, Jesus, he really creamed one at me. And I blocked the ball and the ball kind of hit me in the chest and came up high. And I caught the ball and threw it and I thought I threw him out. The umpire called him safe.

The scoreboard said it was a base hit, and everyone of course knew that his streak was still going. Thornton Lee was pitching. And they tied up the ball game and we went eleven innings. And Joe came up in the eleventh inning and he hit one on the top deck in left center. That erased that doubtful-looking hit.

~

Sportswriters rummaged through record books to determine exactly whom DiMaggio was chasing. The modern National League record was thirty-three games by Rogers Hornsby. The American League record was forty-one by George Sisler.

On June 21, he singled against Detroit's Dizzy Trout to pass Hornsby at thirty-four games.

The nation was starting to notice.

Tommy Henrich:

It built up. It sure did build up. Nobody was concerned when DiMaggio hit in ten games, fifteen games. He did that all the time. Then, when we were aware what the record was, well, the whole country was tuned in by then.

~

Back home in San Francisco, they were tuned in. **Jerry Coleman** *was sixteen that summer:*

I was raised in San Francisco. I knew the DiMaggio story very, very well, because I read it all my life. When he was in that streak in '41, I was a senior in high school. Every day it was a headline story, what he did in that streak. It was a front-page story, every day. His average was on the front page, in a little box, every day.

⌒

In New York, they were tuned in. Baseball fan **Everett Parker**:

All over America, I guess it was going on. Everyone was saying, the people working and what have you, "How did Joe do today? How did Joe do today?" That was the password in 1941.

I was twelve years old and in P.S. 77, a grammar school in Ridgewood, Queens. People would ask in the street, "Hey, how did Joe do today?" It was all over New York.

⌒

On ball fields in small towns, they were tuned in.
Boo Ferriss:

I was in school playing college baseball at Mississippi State University in the summer of '41. That summer, I was playing in the Northern League, a college league in Brattleboro, Vermont. I was up there when all the fanfare was going on. The two big things were DiMaggio's hitting streak and Williams working on being a .400

hitter. I followed it very closely. We all did, mostly through the daily newspapers.

⌒

At Fenway Park, they were tuned in. **Dominic DiMaggio** *was playing center field for the Red Sox that summer, and didn't have to wait long for updates on his brother. They were delivered by Red Sox left fielder Ted Williams:*

I found out immediately about whether he got a hit or not. I would call over to Teddy or Teddy would get it from the scoreboard operator at Fenway Park. And he would yell over to me, "Dommy, Joe got a base hit." That's how I got my information.

⌒

In the last week of June, DiMaggio was closing in on Sisler's forty-one. In the eighth inning of game thirty-eight, against the Saint Louis Browns at Yankee Stadium, DiMaggio was hitless. The Yankees were ahead, 3-1, and he was scheduled to bat fourth in the bottom of the eighth.

If the Yankees were retired in order, the Streak was done.

Red Rolfe led off with a walk, the next batter popped out, and Henrich stepped to the plate with a runner at first and a terrible, awful thought in his head—if he hit into a double play, DiMaggio would not get a chance to hit.

Henrich came up with a drastic solution: bunt.
Henrich:

We didn't play that way. With one out and a man on first and the number-three hitter up, you're supposed to hit a base hit. Not bunt.

I felt that situation coming on. And, you know, I could hit Eldon Auker better than any other pitcher I ever faced in my entire life. I don't even know why. But I still might have hit a screaming line drive at the second baseman and doubled the guy at first.

So I thought about it and I went into the dugout and I went over to Joe (McCarthy) and I said, "Joe, would it be all right if I bunted?"

Now I'll tell you, McCarthy thought about it for about four seconds. And he looked at me and said, "That'll be all right." In other words, he knew exactly what was going on. And why. And DiMaggio hit another line drive.

~

In game forty against the Philadelphia Athletics, DiMaggio faced Johnny Babich, whom the Yankees had traded away in the spring of 1940. Babich carried a healthy grudge against his old team, and vowed to stop DiMaggio, even if it meant walking him every time.

His first time up, DiMaggio walked. His second time up, DiMaggio walked. His third time up, Babich went to 3-0 on him.

The fourth pitch was outside, but not out of reach. DiMaggio lashed it up the middle, between Babich's legs, and into center field. DiMaggio looked back on it as one of his greatest moments.

In the first game of a doubleheader against Washington, DiMaggio tied Sisler. Between games, he got bad news: A reporter had uncovered a forty-four-game hit streak by Wee Willie Keeler before the turn of the century. DiMaggio still had four to go.

To start the second game, he got really bad news: His game bat was missing. Ballplayers, especially those on hot streaks, get attached to a game bat the way a toddler gets attached to a teddy bear. The stoic DiMaggio was near panic.

Tommy Henrich*:*

We were playing a doubleheader down there, in Washington. I think it was a Sunday afternoon. We won the first game and we were inside, cooling off a little bit, changing clothes and so forth. Then we go out to play the second game.

I go up and I'm the number-three hitter. I'm heading for the plate and I hear behind me, "Hey, Tom!" I turned around and DiMaggio was the guy who hollered at me. I start back to him and before I got to him, he says, "You got my bat." I said, "No, Joe, . . ." He said, "Let me see it." He didn't even listen to me.

He took a look at it. It wasn't his bat. Anyway, he went up to hit with another bat. He hit a nice line drive to right-center field and the guy made a good running catch of it. Now, I pass him going to the outfield. And he says, "If that had been my bat, it would have been in there." This is the one that's going to break the record! I knew from then, boy. He is really worried. He knew the importance of the situation.

We get into the dugout and he's looking the bats over. He couldn't find a bat that he said he liked. I said, "Joe, take a look at mine." And he looked at it and he said, "Yeah, it looks pretty good." I said, "Take it." And he wouldn't do it.

Now here's a guy, he's afraid he might break my bat. Isn't that something? So he didn't use it.

I think it was the third time he was up. I said, "Joe, for Pete's sakes. Take my doggone bat. If you like the darn thing, use it." Well, he went out and got a base hit. Now he uses that for a whole week. Lo and behold, over in Newark, in the Italian section, they find out that this young Italian kid had swiped Joe's bat in Washington. The older guys said, "Hey, we gotta get this bat back to Big Joe." So they took the doggone bat back to Yankee Stadium and gave it over to Joe.

George Sisler:

I'd rather see DiMaggio break it than anybody I can think of. That guy's a natural in everything he does and is a great hitter. His streak is no lucky fluke, believe me.[4]

Everywhere he went, the stands were packed, and people were talking about the Streak. Radio announcers broke into regularly scheduled programming to provide updates. Bojangles Robinson danced on the Yankee dugout for luck. The pressure was enormous—millions of people were hanging on each and every at-bat. It was as if DiMaggio were playing Game 7 of the World Series, day after day after day. He took to coming to the ballpark way early, just to sit in the stands and gaze peacefully over the empty field.

Henrich:

He didn't show any pressure. He never talked about it. From what I know of Joe, he wasn't built that way. He never let us in on his inner thoughts or anything. He never said anything.

Jiminy, you've got to realize—he was a tough guy on the ball field!

DiMaggio tied Keeler by hitting in both games of a double-header against the Red Sox at Fenway Park. Game forty-five, the potential record breaker, was against the Red Sox at Yankee Stadium.

In the first inning, Boston left fielder Stan Spence reached over the wall and snatched a home run away from DiMaggio.

In his next at-bat, DiMaggio ripped a line drive to center that looked like a sure hit.

It was caught on a spectacular play by the center fielder, **Dom DiMaggio**:

I recall I did take away a base hit. In retrospect, I wish that I hadn't. I went a long way to steal one from him. So he was hitless at that point.

The next time he came to bat, he hit the ball into the seats so that nobody could catch it this time.

~

On the night of July 17 in Cleveland, the Streak ended at fifty-six when DiMaggio walked his first time up, grounded out twice on great plays deep behind the bag by Indians third baseman Ken Keltner, and grounded into a double play on a hard, tricky hop to shortstop Lou Boudreau.

Baseball fans forever remembered where they were the night DiMaggio's streak ended.

Everett Parker:

I remember when it ended, because that was big news. Before you even had to wait for radio, I remember people on the streets saying, "Hey, geez, it's over. Joe's streak ended."

~

After the game, DiMaggio asked shortstop Phil Rizzuto to accompany him out of the ballpark.

Rizzuto:

Now Joe gets dressed and we walk out of the gate together. He doesn't say a word. We just start walking back toward the Cleveland hotel. We go about two blocks. I don't know what to say to comfort him, so I say nothing.

Finally he looks up at me with a little smile. "Do you know if I got a hit tonight I would have made ten thousand dollars? The Heinz 57 people were following me. They wanted to make some deal with me." Then he reached into his back pocket. "Son of a bitch. I forgot my wallet. I left it in the park. Phil, how much money have you got?" I reached into my pocket and pulled out my wallet. I had eighteen dollars. "Let me have it." I gave it to him and he turned toward a bar. I started in, and he turned back toward me. "No, you go on back to the hotel. I want to relax a bit." I just left him and walked back.[5]

Johnny Sturm, *Yankees first baseman in 1941:*

The funny thing of it was, they were watching my streak before they were watching Joe's. Myself being a rookie, you see. I was hitting in twelve, thirteen, fourteen games in a row. They started following my streak. Nobody noticed it until Dan Daniel, one of the New York sportswriters, started following it. It got to be about sixteen, seventeen games. And then Vince called a newspaper guy—I don't know who the hell he called—

and he said, "Do you guys realize that Joe has got a streak going?" That's what set them on Joe's streak.

We got to Washington. I think I was at sixteen or seventeen. We got rained out in the second game of a doubleheader. I didn't get a hit and the game was called because of rain. Joe got his hit in his last time up before it rained. He got a hit and it got counted. From then on, that's when they all started getting in on Joe's streak.

It was a funny thing about that streak. A lot of guys played it down. In fact, our ball club didn't get enthused over it. The reason why was, the Big Dago always got his hit in his first at-bat, or the second time at bat. It didn't often get down to the last time at bat. He always seemed to get his hit in the first or second time at bat. That helped our team, you know

As far as myself, Red Rolfe, and Tommy Henrich, we knew that the streak was going on after twenty, twenty-five games. I was leading off all the time. Hell, I had to keep taking, taking, taking all the time. I had to try to get on base as much as I could, being the leadoff man.

The old man, McCarthy, told me what I had to do when I got up there. He said, "Take a pitch. If that's a ball, take another pitch." He had me up there swinging with two strikes all the time. It seemed I was always up there with two strikes. You give those pitchers two strikes, and they got you. McCarthy's idea was, "John, if I can get them to throw fifteen or twenty pitches to you, by the fifth inning, that fastball of theirs was gone. The rest of these boys, DiMaggio, will knock them off."

Trying to get a walk or to get hit by the ball. Red Rolfe had to do the same thing. But Tommy Henrich was hitting third all the time, and it was up to him a lot of times to get Joe going. I think there was more pressure on Tommy Henrich than anybody during the Streak. Because we needed to save Joe another at-bat. We always had to try to get Joe another at-bat, and Tommy Henrich was the last guy up before Joe. But generally, Joe always had that hit or two before it came to that, that fourth or fifth time at bat.

We didn't hardly talk about it. I don't know. The Yankees were a funny ball club. They were a real close-knit team. The Yankees were real close-knit. But talking about any individual stuff—very seldom did they do that kind of talk. They'd play their game and go home to the wife and kids. And that's what the setup was. The next day, we'd come and play again. It was very seldom that anybody would talk about "I this" or "I that." There was hardly anything like that. Very little discussion on the club about the Streak.

I'll tell you what, he never showed any pressure. He never did show it. He was just like everybody else. He didn't say anything about a streak or anything else. He'd just go out and play his ball game.

He'd talk about the kind of things we all talked about. He was going out with those show people and that. He'd said, "I had to get dressed two or three different times last night." He'd come home and he'd be sleeping, and his wife would come in with a bunch of show people and he'd have to get up and change clothes. Hell, he'd be up to two or three o'clock in the morning sometimes.

Every now and then he'd break down and talk a little bit. He was always a very exclusive, a very good dresser. He always had to wear his trousers a certain way. He always had to wear suspenders with trousers. He'd talk a little about that. But very seldom would he talk about baseball.

I guess I can remember the end of the Streak better than anything. Well, that Keltner. I knew Keltner when he was with Minneapolis. He had a terrific arm and he was a helluva good fielder. He was a great big-league ballplayer, that Keltner. And he had his own idea about Joe DiMaggio.

When Joe got up at bat, Keltner went all the way back to the outfield grass. And right close to the line. He wasn't but two or three feet away from the line. And Joe hit a scorcher the first time at bat. It should have been a hit. He just nipped him at first base. It was as close as the thinnest piece of paper. The umpire could have called it either way. The next time up, that damn same identical thing happened again. A lot of times the guys used to say, "Hell, why doesn't Joe lay a bunt down? With Keltner playing that far back, he could walk to first base." That's what one or two guys said. But Joe never did. Keltner just took two damn good hits away from him. They should have been doubles. Hit down the line. I would give Keltner a lot of credit for playing the position the way he did.

The one to Boudreau? That was just a regular hit. It kind of bounced up on him a little bit. Big-league ballplayers in those days, that sort of thing didn't bother them too much. It bounced off his chest a little. But it was a double play. That was it. It was Keltner's deal. That took the cake that night.

There was nothing said. Our guys just said, "Joe, you had a good streak." And let it go at that. You know it had to end sometime. That's what Joe said. "I knew it had to end sometime." That was about the conversation. Some guys have tried to make it seem like he was depressed. I don't think that happened.

～

On August 29, 1941, the Yankees checked into the Hotel Shoreham in Washington, D.C. Roommates Lefty Gomez and Joe DiMaggio were headed out for dinner when Gomez said, "I just remembered something, Joe. I've got to go by Selkirk's room down the hall here." Gomez dragged DiMaggio with him and in room 609D found something special.

Johnny Sturm *remembers:*

We had a little party. It was just a get-together. All the ballplayers got together. Bill Dickey organized it. The idea was to give Joe something, to reward him for something that he did. Everybody was there. We gave Joe a humidor. I think they got it from Tiffany's. I think they paid four hundred dollars for the thing, or something like that. It was solid silver. You couldn't have much of a party in a little room. Joe was surprised. Joe was always smoking cigarettes. He said, "Oh, this will come in handy." We all had our signatures engraved in the thing. We just wanted to give him a little something.

～

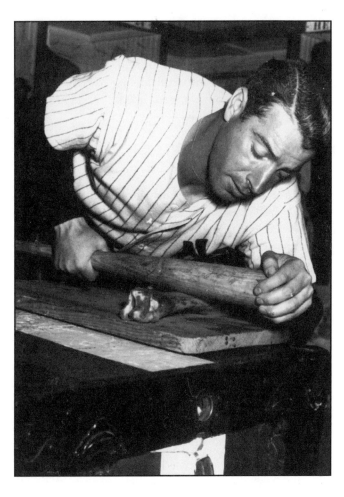

Even though he transcended mere superstar status, DiMaggio was not above boning his own bats, as he does here during spring training in 1950. (AP/Wide World Photos)

THE GREAT DiMAGGIO

"More than any ballplayer, I never saw a guy bear down, day after day, pitch after pitch, supreme—oh, my golly—the pride that he had. Playing like a pro, never dog it, never relaxed. I don't know how his body could stand it."

—TOMMY HENRICH

Joe DiMaggio chased perfection on the ball field and nearly caught up with it. He was intense. He was dedicated. He was proud of his work. He was like a singer who didn't want to hit a single bad note, a writer who didn't want to type a single bad sentence.

His game was part science, part art. He was a gifted athlete—he could run, field, throw, hit for average, and hit for power. And he was a smart ballplayer—he ran the bases with skill, hit the cutoff man, outthought the other side.

While he was making it look easy, he worked terribly hard. He paid for his perfectionism. On the field, he was quietly dignified, stoic, graceful and all that, the stuff that impressed Hemingway's fisherman in *The Old Man and the Sea*. But the fear, the nerves, the emotion had to go somewhere. Off the field, he guzzled coffee, chain-smoked Camels and Chesterfields, and nursed ulcers.

"Nobody ever worked harder than I did," DiMaggio said in a burble of candor in 1976. "And effortless? Let me tell you, every time I take a step today I am reminded of my baseball career. My body aches all over from all that it took to play this game."[1]

~

Jimmy Cannon wrote it, and hundreds have since quoted, misquoted, and paraphrased the DiMaggio creed on giving it all, all the time. Yankee teammate **Jerry Coleman**'s *version:*

What you've heard is absolutely true. In a 15-3 game, the ninth inning, and he's running around like a lunatic, sliding, jumping, this and that. You'd say, "Joe, take it easy."

He said, "Yeah, but there might be somebody here who's never seen me play before." That's a true story. That's the way he was.

~

The Great DiMaggio

That's the way he played, whether the games counted or not. DiMaggio was in the army 1943–45, unhappily entertaining troops in exhibition baseball games in the United States and in Hawaii.

Dario Lodigiani *remembers him in those games:*

I was in the service with Joe. We were stationed in Hawaii at Hickam Field. Joe played hard over there. He was bearing down over there. Man, he put a big show on for those people.

Joe's theory was that a lot of people had heard of him, but a lot of people had never seen him play. He wasn't going to play lackadaisical. Whatever the people thought of him, their first impression was a good one.

⌒

When the Great DiMaggio and his accompanying Yankees came to town, it was like the circus had rolled in. DiMaggio knew people hate to be disappointed when they go to the circus. He knew there was no such thing as a meaningless game.

Baseball fan **Vernon Feen** *remembers an exhibition match in Columbus, Ohio, in the spring of 1946:*

I was in the seventh grade. Here we had an exhibition game between the Brooklyn Dodgers and the New York Yankees. We were excited. DiMaggio was my number one baseball hero. From the time when I was ten or eleven until I was twenty-one or twenty-two, baseball was everything to me.

The game was on a Wednesday. We wanted to go. I did, and some of my friends. I wasn't sure how we were going to do it. I had never missed school. The thought went through my head that maybe I'd have a funeral to go to that day.

Before school started, I went to the office. I had never been to the office before. I was probably afraid to go there. Mr. Huber was the principal. I said, "Mr. Huber, the New York Yankees are playing the Brooklyn Dodgers today out at Redbird Stadium. And we'd like to go."

He checked our grades. We were all good students. He excused us. There were at least two or three other guys that I knew about that cut school that day. They wanted to go to the ball game, too. He paddled them the next day when they came back.

DiMaggio played a great game. He had a double, a shot off the right-center-field fence. He had three sharp singles. The only time he made an out, he hit a 430-foot shot to left field.

Then, Carl Furillo was on first base. A low liner was hit to center field. DiMaggio, it seemed effortlessly—he was there. And he just kind of made a quick flip to first base and the ball skidded in there on one hop, and Furillo was out. He was as smooth as silk. I was there to see Joe DiMaggio, and he didn't let me down.

THE GREAT DIMAGGIO

DiMaggio knew what he owed himself and the paying customers. Yankee teammate **Jerry Coleman***:*

It was in spring training 1948. He had blisters all over his hands. Joe was not a guy who did a lot in the off-season. I looked at his hands one day, and there were these big blisters. And he went right through it. Some people would take a day off. Joe would never stop.

He didn't play much in the spring. But he made every trip. That was one thing he had to do, as *the* guy on the ball club. No matter where we went or how long it took, he was on the trip, and he'd pinch-hit if he didn't play.

⌒

There was only one way to play baseball. Yankee teammate **Tommy Henrich** *recalls how DiMaggio made sure younger players knew it:*

It's not that Joe was a leader. All you had to do was follow what he did. He never preached, "Hey, you didn't run that out." I never heard him say anything like that. But I'll tell you, one look from him, and if you were a rookie and you were guilty of not hustling, a look from him was enough. He'd stare you down. You'd cringe.

More than any ballplayer, I never saw a guy bear down, day after day, pitch after pitch, supreme—oh, my golly—the pride that he had. Playing like a pro, never dog it, never relaxed. I don't know how his body could stand it.

The ball game is over, and he still wasn't a barrel of fun in the clubhouse. That was his nature. That's the kind of guy that he was. He never relaxed in anything he did.

~

Jimmy Rego remembers testing DiMaggio's pride:

In '38, Joe held out. I pitched for the Seals in 1938. I was in spring training with them down in Hanford. Down there by Fresno. My manager was Lefty O'Doul. He said, "Listen, we're going to have Joe down here for a couple of weeks because he's holding out. He's holding out and he wants to work out with us." He wasn't in spring training with the Yankees.

He came out and worked out with us. O'Doul says, "I want you to throw batting practice to him." They wanted a left-handed pitcher to throw to him.

So I throw Joe batting practice. And boy he's hitting shots off of me. Christ, four or five hundred feet! My catcher at that time was Eddie Bothello. I told Eddie, I says, "Hey, Jesus Christ, O'Doul wants me to throw batting practice to Joe. And he's up there hitting shots off of me, five hundred feet! I'm trying to make this ball club and this guy is hitting me like he owns me. He looks like Babe Ruth out there!"

I said, "You know what I'm going to do, Eddie? Be ready. I'm going to go in there and I'm going to throw a little hard." So I'm throwing hard. So Joe tells Eddie,

"What the hell is that left-hander doing out there? Does he think he's pitching a ball game? This is only batting practice."

So Eddie, the catcher, comes out to me and he says, "Jim. Joe is kind of pissed off. He says you're throwing that god——ed ball like you're pitching a ball game." I said, "Listen, I'm trying to make this ball club. When they see this guy hitting five-hundred-foot home runs, how am I going to make the ball club? Listen, you tell Joe that I'm going to cut loose a little."

And, Jesus, I was throwing hard and shoving the bat right up his ass. He was so pissed off. He threw the bat halfway out to the mound. He said, "You sonofabitch, what are you trying to do, pitch a ball game?" I said, "No. But it sure looks like it, doesn't it?" And he walked off the diamond.

⌒

DiMaggio was a can-do player. Somehow, one way or another, he got the job done. Long before Nike, DiMaggio owned the slogan: Just do it.

His brother **Dominic** *remembers that was true even on the sandlots of San Francisco:*

We played on the North Beach playground as kids. We played a lot of baseball, touch-tackle football. Joe was always much taller and bigger than I was. He played in these contests and I, because I was much smaller, was on the sidelines. So I remember watching him.

I recall in a touch-tackle football game, he was always the quarterback. He was pretty good at that, too. There was a fellow named Louis Daresta. He later became an all-American football player.

During a particular touch-tackle football game, you had to touch the guy with two hands with the ball to get him down. During the early part of the game, Joe had done something to embarrass Louis somewhat. I don't recall exactly what it was.

But a little bit later in the game, Louis, who was a tough little football player, was running interference for the guy who had the ball. And the only one left between them was Joe.

Louis felt he was going to take a shot at Joe. So he bent down low and started after Joe as if to knock his legs out from under him.

And Joe held his ground and the runner was right behind Louis. When Louis got to Joe, Joe just gingerly bounced back a little and with both his hands, hit Louis on the back. And because Louis was down so far, he lost balance. He fell and skinned both knees. All torn up. Of course, this was on a tar field.

And Joe reached over Louis and touched, with two hands, the ball carrier.

＿＿＿

In 1933, 1934, and 1935, the once-mighty Yankees did not win the pennant. In 1936, DiMaggio came up and New York returned to the World Series against the Giants. The Yankees won in six games.

THE GREAT DiMAGGIO

*Losing manager **Bill Terry**, a coldly analytical type, picked apart the series and assessed the new world champions, who included Bill Dickey, Red Rolfe, Tony Lazzeri, Frank Crosetti, Red Ruffing, and Lefty Gomez:*

I'd like to add one thing. I've always heard that one player could make the difference between a losing team and a winner, and I never believed it. Now I know it's true.[2]

(Of course, he was talking about DiMaggio.)

*Red Sox manager **Joe Cronin**, after DiMaggio's rookie season:*

That DiMaggio has upset the entire balance of the league. If we'd landed him, we'd have won. The Tigers would have repeated if they'd got him. The Indians would be champions if they had him. It was a well-matched league until he came along. He's made the Yankees a powerhouse.[3]

Jim Hubley, baseball fan and longtime writer for the York (Pa.) Daily Record, *twice saw DiMaggio play at Philadelphia's Shibe Park. The sightings were nine years apart, once against the Philadelphia Athletics and once against the Phillies, and the circumstances were drastically different, but DiMaggio's impact was exactly the same.*

59

I Remember Joe DiMaggio

Hubley:

This was August 1941. I was twenty-six. My friend and I had a chance to go down to the game. We were baseball addicts. I was a baseball nut. Let me tell you, whatever ambitions I had then about playing baseball faded when I watched him play. He didn't run, you know—he glided. Beautiful. All they said about him was true.

Anyway, he had gotten in a little slump. He didn't take batting practice that day. My friend and I were really upset, because we had come to see him.

He did play, of course. I don't know, his first three, four times at bat. I know he hit into at least one double play, and struck out—he didn't get a hit. The last time up for him was in the ninth inning. If you know sports, you know how the Philadelphia fans are. They were the same way then. They booed him. But it was sort of a boo of affection.

They didn't have a big crowd there. Way out in left field, there was a guy sitting there all alone. His arms are stretched out. And Joe hit one. The ball landed right on that guy's right side, that seat. He nonchalantly picked up the ball. Maybe it woke him up, I don't know. It was as if Joe said, "I'll hit it to that guy up there." The Yankees won the game.

Nine years later, in the 1950 World Series, it was a little different. There were more people there. Of course, we're rooting for the Phillies. It was the second game. Allie Reynolds was pitching for New York and Robin Roberts was pitching for the Phillies. Anyway, Joe had the same kind of day. I think he actually hit into two double plays. DiMaggio—nothing. I know he struck out at least once. And they were booing.

The thing that impressed me was, he didn't have a hit. He didn't do a thing. But when the score was tied, he came up in the tenth inning, and that crowd was silent. To me, that showed the respect that they showed him, and the fear that he was going to do something. And he hit the ball, and I swear the damn thing landed in the same place that it did nine years earlier. I don't know if it was the same guy sitting there or not.

Exhibition game or World Series game, he was always Joe DiMaggio, but maybe a little more so in the big moments, in the big games, against the toughest pitchers.
Tommy Henrich:

Most of the time when the three of us were in a ball game, I batted number three, DiMag was four, and Keller was five. Charlie Keller, I heard him say this several times, he said, "The best part of DiMaggio I ever saw was the battles he had with Bobby Feller."

There were a lot of right-handers who hated to bat against Feller, because he had a lack of control with all that good stuff. When Joe would go to home plate, here was the doggone pride of DiMaggio. "I'm not going to look bad against you. I don't care how good you are." Charlie said he could see the veins in Joe's neck when he was up there. That was nothing but pride, in my book.

I Remember Joe DiMaggio

Former Saint Louis Browns first baseman **Chuck Stevens**:

Everybody was in awe of him in tough situations. He'd walk to the plate, and you'd know, if you got him out, what an accomplishment. To get him out, particularly in a jam, was a major accomplishment.

Yankees teammate **Bobby Brown**:

He could just rise. He had another gear that he could get into in big games, and late in the game. He could just do things that you didn't think anybody could do.

He could go from home to second faster than anyone I ever saw. He could make a long single into a double. He could go from first to third and from second to home faster than anyone I ever saw, if it was a big run. He did all those little things.

He could hit good pitching in big games. And you've got a lot of guys who can't do that.

Yankees teammate **Johnny Murphy**:

I remember many a day Joe would be the third hitter in a close game and McCarthy would call him back. "Now

Joe," he'd say, "don't forget, I'd rather you hit a ball over your head than get a base on balls because you can drive that run in, even on bad balls over your head. So don't get a base on balls." And Joe never did. He'd swing at many bad balls to get a run in, and wouldn't think anything about it.[4]

*Yankees teammate **Eddie Lopat**:*

If he went oh-for-four and we lost, he'd sit there in front of his locker for thirty, forty minutes and never move. He'd felt he'd let the club down. No man can carry a club by himself. But that's just the way he felt. He hadn't done the job that day. He'd let his teammates down.[5]

Of course, he hated the idea of failing in big moments, not getting the job done, losing big games. DiMaggio's Yankees just didn't do that sort of thing.

During his thirteen seasons in New York, DiMaggio played in ten World Series. The Yankees lost only one of them, in 1942 to the Cardinals.

Another October story:

In the 1947 World Series, the Yankees wrestled hard with the Brooklyn Dodgers. In Game 4, New York right-hander Bill Bevens was one out from the first World Series no-hitter—and the Yankees were one out from a 3-games-to-1 lead in the series.

Then Dodgers pinch hitter Cookie Lavagetto doubled home two runs to win the game.

The next afternoon, the Yankees were leading, 2-1, in the ninth. The Dodgers had a runner on with one out.

Cookie Lavagetto walked to the on-deck circle.

Tommy Henrich *recalls DiMaggio's will to win:*

Somebody hit a fly ball to right-center field. It was a lazy fly ball. It was a little closer to me and I called for it. Now we need one more out to win. We know that Lavagetto is going to be the pinch hitter again.

We need one more out. We were wondering if Lavagetto could do it again. I threw the ball in and DiMaggio said to me, "For Chrissake, say a prayer." (Frank) Shea struck out Lavagetto and the game is over. Now we're naturally elated.

We go into the clubhouse and it's a madhouse in there. Frank Crosetti is close to me and I say, "Frank, listen to this." I relayed to Frank exactly what happened, of the great DiMaggio saying, "For Chrissake, say a prayer." Believe me, it wasn't in a vulgar way. I told Crosetti the story and his reaction was, he looked right at me and says, "Why didn't you tell *him* to pray."

Now, I think that's pretty good. So I got up and walked over to Joe. I said, "Hey, this is what Crosetti had to say about you."

DiMaggio says, "I was praying. But I wasn't sure if I was getting through or not."

Brothers and on-field rivals Vince and Joe DiMaggio meet prior to an exhibition game in 1937. (AP/Wide World Photos)

Dario Lodigiani, *DiMaggio's boyhood chum, was playing infield for the White Sox when he encountered his friend's combative streak:*

Joe was a competitor. He played hard. Boy, and I was an infielder. I broke in as a second baseman. There were times when he went into me and I thought a truck ran over me. That's the way he played. Even if you were close friends, he was playing to win.

~

Jerry Coleman *saw it, too:*

Against the Red Sox, Johnny Pesky took out Rizzuto. It was a tough slide. Just barreled him. I don't know if it was on purpose or whatever.

So the next inning, DiMaggio came up and hit a single to left field. He never stopped. He went into second and took Doerr into left field. And that kind of thing, when you're a young player, you think, *Oooooh. Wow. That's our guy.*

~

Jimmy Cannon wrote that no one who saw DiMaggio play ever forgot the sight. That was true in 1933, when he signed with the San Francisco Seals, and baseball fans up and down the Pacific Coast League picked up impressions that lasted into the next century.

THE GREAT DIMAGGIO

Johnny Pesky, *future major-leaguer with the Boston Red Sox, remembers when the Seals came to play the hometown Portland Beavers:*

I was one of the little kids hanging around the ballpark. When you're ten, twelve, the impressions were made. He looked like the ultimate successful player. You could see that.

He was a guy who you could just go to the ballpark and just watch what he did and how he did it. Even before the game. You could see he was special.

⌒

Lee Stine *pitched for the Seals in the early 1930s:*

He played the last two days in the '32 season. He had a brother, Vince. An older brother. That whole year, Vince was there. Something happened to the shortstop we had. It was Augie Galan. So we needed a shortstop to play Saturday and Sunday. That'd be three games—a doubleheader on Sunday.

So Vince said that he had a younger brother who could fill the bill. So our manager said, "Okay, bring him out tomorrow, bring him out."

So Joe came out and he played shortstop. He got a couple of hits. Hit one up against the left-field fence. Seals Stadium was like a big airport, you know.

Sunday, he played the doubleheader and got three or four hits. You could see he had the great natural ability, even then.

Louis Almada:

I played for the Mission Reds. I played center field. When DiMaggio came out of high school, he came out there that summer to try out for the Seals. Ike Caveney was managing the Seals then. Joe had been playing shortstop over at Galileo. He charged a couple of balls. He booted a couple of balls. Caveney took him out after the seventh or eighth inning.

The next day, he put him in right field. What he was impressed with was the strength, the tremendous hands he had. The speed of his bat.

Almada recalls watching DiMaggio bloom under the guidance of Caveney's successor on the Seals, Lefty O'Doul.

Lefty O'Doul was a great hitter himself. He hit .398 one year with Brooklyn. Anyway, he told Joe to spread his feet out. Hit off his back foot. He said, "Don't move until you see the ball. Just wait until the ball gets on top of you. Hold your bat back. Hold your bat up high." O'Doul had to correct a few things. Joe didn't just fall into it right away. But you could see that tremendous change that came over him.

Joe hurt his knee. Charlie Graham was a great guy. He was the owner of the Seals. The sportswriters knew that Joe was a great prospect. They gave him some infield hits when somebody booted one. Just to keep him at .300, when he was hurt. But as soon as that swelling went down, the Yankees bought him for $25,000. They would have had to pay $125,000 at least, if he hadn't got hurt. The other clubs could see how this guy was developing. But Charlie wasn't sure about the knee. He needed the money. So when they offered him that money, he took it.

In 1935, Oscar Eckhardt was hitting around .398. Joe was hitting around .330. Joe went up into the .390s. He hit something like .500 for the last two months of the season.

Joe blossomed into such a great hitter. Eckhardt was hitting around .398, .397. DiMaggio was at .388, .389. Oscar beat him by one or two points. Joe made up ten points at the end. DiMaggio would have caught him if he had one more day. The last day, I think Eckhardt had four hits and DiMaggio had six. He just missed beating him. But of course, Joe was a much better hitter.

Joe could go get a ball. He had that knack of not looking. Just hearing the crack of the bat and taking off. Just gliding back there. It seemed like he had radar. He would get that jump on the ball and just take a long stride. He never seemed to need a big effort. Then he'd glide into the ball or stretch out. I never saw him dive for a ball. He always seemed to be there. And if he couldn't be there, it was because it was impossible.

They compare Ted Williams to DiMaggio. When Ted Williams dropped his bat, you couldn't compare him to DiMaggio in any way, shape, or form. DiMaggio could outrun him, outthrow him, outthink him, out everything. At least that's what I think.

Joe helped Ted Williams. When he saw Ted Williams, he saw such a fast bat. He told Ted the same thing he was told. He said, "Ted, spread your legs out." Ted was hitting home runs down there in San Diego. He was keeping his legs close together and winding up. He told him to spread his legs out and get his bat back. Just wait for the ball to get on top of you. And then hit. Don't worry about the gyrations that the pitcher uses. Wait for that ball to leave his hand.

Jimmy Rego:

I did a lot of pitching against old Joe. My first year with the Coast League was with Oakland in 1934. Joe was with the Seals. We used to play against each other a lot.

By golly, pitching one game against him, I beat the Seals, and I was told I was the only guy who ever struck him out three times in one game. I was just out of high school. He was considered a helluva prospect.

Billy Raimondi was our catcher. I kind of got pissed off at Billy because him and DiMaggio were very close friends. He was tipping off Joe. He was telling him what I was throwing. And God bless, it didn't help him any. I was able to get him out. When I pitched to him, I gave it a little extra. I was thinking, *This guy is tough. I'm going to have to work on him.*

The Great DiMaggio

⌒

His being special was true even in 1936, when DiMaggio joined the Yankees.

Future teammate **Bobby Brown** *was in the stands:*

I lived in New Jersey from the seventh grade until halfway through my sophomore year of high school. When I was in the East, I saw the 1936 and 1937 World Series and saw him play in those. I saw him play in a number of regular season games in the late thirties.

He was a terrific player. You just knew that he played awfully well and that he was the best player out there.

⌒

It was true in 1937, when **Henrich** *joined DiMaggio in the New York outfield:*

He made a wonderful play the first year I was there. In Cleveland. A fly ball to right-center field, and he was on the move and caught the ball, and without pivoting he threw the guy out at third base. The guy had tagged up at second. I don't know how Joe put the brakes on so that he could get any leverage on that ball. But he did. I saw that and I said, "Hey, man. He's Superman."

⌒

I Remember Joe DiMaggio

*One of the twentieth century's healthiest egotists, **Ted Williams**, freely admitted he envied Joe DiMaggio:*

I never, ever compared myself to him. I thought there never was a greater player in the history of baseball. For me just to be mentioned in the same breath, boy, I always felt like I was two steps below him. I thought I could hit with anybody, but he was in my opinion as good as any that ever played this game. There's only one guy I saw you could mention in the same breath, and that was Willie Mays. I felt that just to have my name mentioned with Joe, it elevated me. I never thought I was ever as good.[6]

~

Johnny Sturm, *DiMaggio's teammate on the '41 Yankees:*

Joe never seemed to be out of condition. He was always in the same condition. Except one time, he hurt his arm. He had hurt his arm swinging the bat. The next day, he said he was going to try to throw it out. That's what he said. "I'm going to throw it out." So he threw the ball over home plate one time, he threw the ball over home plate twice. I think if you look back, that was the only time he had two or three errors in a ball game. They were all throwing errors.

~

THE GREAT DiMAGGIO

Hall of Fame second baseman **Bobby Doerr** *of the Red Sox played against DiMaggio for twelve seasons in the big leagues:*

Joe DiMaggio was a perfect ballplayer. He had a great arm, great range in the outfield, because he could accelerate so quick from a standing position. I thought Ted (Williams) was probably a shade better hitter, but Joe was right there. Don't forget, Joe played in the toughest ballpark in the American League to hit in. You had the long left field, white shirts in the background in those days, the shadows from the tall stands. I just thought it was a heckuva place to have to hit in, back when we had day ball.

When you look at that record of fifty-six straight, he only struck out thirteen times that year. For a guy with power, a dead-pull hitter, you have to be so precise to do that.

He beat you in so many ways. His baserunning. He could have stolen thirty to forty bases a year if they'd let him. He did it in the Coast League. I played against him in 1935 in the Coast League. He was so good.

I got him in a rundown one time, which really woke me up to the fact as to why he was such a great outfielder. I was just right close to him and I had the ball. It was a rundown between first and second. He took off and I just barely tagged him. Boy, that quickly made me realize that he could accelerate from a standing position. And that's why he was such a great outfielder.

He had the legs, the arm, and the instincts to be a great outfielder, and he had a good mind for it. DiMaggio played smart.

Is there anything more stupid in sports than major-league outfielders crashing, careening, and crunching into one another?

Tommy Henrich, *who played alongside him in the outfield for ten seasons:*

DiMaggio and I never once came close to bumping into each other. I see outfielders running into each other, or the second baseman and an outfielder bumping each other. Guys say, "Did you ever have any trouble with DiMaggio?" I say, "No. We had a system." This sounds great, doesn't it? We had a system.

"What was your system?" If I wanted the ball, I called for it. DiMaggio gave it to me.

If I didn't want the ball, I got out of the way. Because it ain't gonna drop. DiMaggio's gonna catch it. He knew he could go all out, because I wasn't going to interfere with him.

Let me give you an example. I liked to pull a trapped ball trick in the big leagues. If I got a dummy on second base, and somebody on first base, and they hit it out to me, I'd trap the ball and we'd get two outs out of it. One day, we're playing this ball club and I'm saying, "Oh, hit it out here." I had the perfect guy on second base.

And he didn't hit it out to me. He hit a lazy fly ball to short center field. And I take off for it. And when I thought I could get to the point where I could get to the ball to trap it, I called for the ball. Now, DiMaggio is standing there. That's how easy the ball was going to be for him to catch. But I called for the ball. So he let me have it.

I'm running now from right to center and naturally my body is not facing the ball as it comes down. The ball is coming down on my left side. I got there in time to trap the ball sideways. I knocked it down and it rolled away about five feet and I jumped on it as fast as I could and I looked down at second base and there's my dummy, still standing there. So we got a double play again.

The point I'm making is, that DiMaggio backed off a ball that was a cinch for him because I called for it. That proved that our system worked.

⁓

Eddie Lopat pitched for the Yankees with DiMaggio behind him in center field from 1948 through 1951:

I was pitching against Cleveland in Yankee Stadium and we're ahead, 3-2. It's about the fifth or sixth inning and Boudreau's the hitter. I sorta turned around to center field, trying to make up my mind what I wanted to start Boudreau with, and I noticed Joe was playing Boudreau straight away in dead center.

So I turned around, got the sign, threw my pitch, and it was a ball. So I turned around to center again to think what I was gonna do with the next pitch and DiMag is still in dead center, and I went back to the rubber and got the sign and missed again. Now I'm 2-0 and really peeved, and this time I don't turn around. On the next pitch Boudreau hits a frozen rope over Rizzuto's head right in the gap and as I turned to follow the ball, I'm thinking, "Oh, my God, there goes a triple at least." As I followed the ball out to the outfield, Joe was standing right there. Never moved. I was shocked. So when the inning was over, I went over and sat down next to him. "Joe," I said, "I noticed on the first two pitches to Boudreau you were playing dead center. How the hell did you get over in the hole waiting for the ball?"

He says, "Well, I seen you pitch enough to know if you were even up or ahead of him, you wouldn't let him pull the ball. But when you got behind two balls and no strikes, I just moved over seventy, eighty feet in the hole."

That's when I said to myself, "Now I know what makes that guy great."[7]

Gil McDougald played third base and second base for the Yankees during DiMaggio's final season:

The one year I had with him, Joe was having his worst year. In 1951. He wasn't too happy. His arm was shot. He couldn't throw. So Phil (Rizzuto) and I, if there were anybody on base, we'd go out deeper than normal to get a cutoff throw from him.

The thing that amazed me was when I was playing second base, with peripheral vision, I could see Joe moving before the ball was even hit. To me, that's a great tip-off on somebody who really knows how to play the outfield. Because most outfielders just stand there. Joe must have known every hitter very well.

⌒

DiMaggio could talk about running after and catching fly balls the way Ted Williams talked about hitting.

Sam Suplizio, *longtime major-league coach and out-field instructor, grew up admiring DiMaggio. In the spring of 1956, he was a Yankee prospect. Manager Casey Stengel took him aside one day during spring training and advised him to learn center field from somebody who really knew his stuff:*

I was invited into the instructional camp, which was the pre-camp to the Yankees' regular spring training. It was held in Saint Petersburg. Since he was retired, they had to push on Joe DiMaggio to get him into camp. I can remember Stengel and them talking: "He's a hard man to get." But he came in for a few days, and he lectured to all the guys in the outfield. Believe me, he looked seven foot tall. It was like he was seven foot tall, and I was a midget. He was like God, and I was a sinner.

He could talk to you about outfield play like a professor. Brilliant. But amazingly, off the field, he didn't say anything. He was very quiet. Almost unapproachable. When you saw him in a hotel, you didn't bother him. You just didn't want anything to do with that.

Listening to him talk about how your feet go in the direction of the ball. Things I used for thirty-five years in the major leagues teaching outfield play. I taught Robin Yount center field in Milwaukee. Rick Manning, Jimmy Edmonds. I taught all those guys. A lot of his stuff, I wrote it all down, because I always wanted to coach. Almost immediately after the practices, I wrote it all down. On a piece of scratch paper. I typed them later on.

From DiMaggio's teaching, a couple of things come to mind right away. One of the finest things he taught me was, when you go back on a ball, to your left, right, or straight over your head, your feet should never side-step. They should go like a track man, in the direction of the ball. Keep the ball off your shoulder, so you don't reach directly over your head for the ball.

I learned how to go back on a ball. I learned how to throw out a runner tagging at a base by playing through a ball and catching it on your throwing side—with two hands. Two hands control the ball when you take it out of your glove. Don't catch it with one and bring it to your throwing hand.

I learned how to practice getting jumps on the ball by coming set and just working on the first three, four, five steps, breaking on balls even though they weren't hit to you. He called it getting out of the box. He got out of his tracks so fast.

He said something, and it makes sense today, more than ever. He said, "When you break, you break clean and quick. You run fast and smooth." These things stayed with me for years.

But your feet going in the direction of the ball—I use that every year. Chad Curtis said to me one day, "I never heard of that. And it's helped me immensely." Luis Polonia, too.

Every time I used it, I told them, "This comes from DiMaggio—the greatest center fielder who ever played the game."

Then there was his hitting. Left-hander **Mel Parnell** *joined the big leagues with the Red Sox in 1947. He recalls veteran hurler Bill Zuber tutoring him on how to deal with the Great DiMaggio:*

I was a rookie, and I was sitting in the bullpen. Bill Zuber told me when DiMaggio came to the plate, "See this guy? Kid, don't ever throw him a changeup. Because if you throw him a changeup, it'll go up there." And he pointed to the upper deck in Yankee Stadium.

So as the game progressed, word comes out to the bullpen for Zuber to warm up. And first thing you know he's in the ball game.

He throws the changeup to DiMaggio and it went right up there, where he said it would.

Zuber goes into the dugout and butts his head on the wall and says, "Dumb Dutchman. Dumb Dutchman. I told the kid not to do it, and I did it."

The Yankee Clipper lays on one of his patented toothy smiles for the cameras in 1946. (AP/Wide World Photos)

THE GREAT DiMAGGIO

DiMaggio's allure was never in the numbers, but he did put together masterpiece seasons. He hit .398 in his last season with the Seals. He hit .346 with forty-six homers and 167 RBIs in 1937 with the Yankees.

He hit .381 in 1939. He hit thirty-nine home runs in 1948.

Now and then, DiMaggio thought about numbers, too.

Bobby Doerr remembers a rare admission from the DiMaggio in his old age:

He told me one time, I guess this was maybe fifteen years ago. We were in Toronto to a banquet up there. Joe said, "Come on, let's go sit down." So we sit down in the lobby there. I said, "Joe, in '35, I remember you having about as good a year as anybody could have."

He said, "Yeah, well. I thought my year of 1939 was probably the best." He said he was hitting around .412 with about three weeks or so to go in the season. He got an infection in his left eye to where he practically had to face the pitcher to look out of his right eye to see the ball. He said he never could understand why McCarthy kept playing him. He said, "We had the pennant cinched. I should have hit .400 that year. But Joe McCarthy insisted that I play."

He said, "I just couldn't see the ball. I never could understand why he made me stay in the lineup."

I don't think he ever said that to too many people.

I Remember Joe DiMaggio

DiMaggio hit 361 lifetime home runs. Baseball dreamers like to wonder what might have been had he played his home games somewhere other than Yankee Stadium, which was preposterously deep in left-center field (457 feet) and center field (461 feet). DiMaggio once looked back and declared he could have hit seventy homers in 1937 if he had played at a different home park.

Hall of Fame left-hander **Whitey Ford**, *who played the 1950 season with DiMaggio:*

If he had not played in Yankee Stadium, he probably would have hit six hundred home runs. There's no telling how many home runs he would have hit had he played in Ebbets Field. I remember as a kid seeing DiMaggio go one-for-eight in the Stadium. He hit a double and he hit seven fly balls that were outs and every one of them went over four hundred feet.[8]

~

Veteran baseball writer **Jack Lang**:

I covered the Yankees from 1958 to 1961. I was with the *Long Island Press*. The more I covered the Yankees at Yankee Stadium, the more respect I had for him, even though he was retired.

When I saw all those long balls that were hit to left-center field, Death Valley as they called it, they would have been home runs in any other ballpark. In the years that he played, he must have hit three hundred balls out in that area that were caught as long flies. I realized what a home run total he would have had if he played in a ball-park with fairer fences. If DiMaggio had played in Fenway Park, he would have hit nine hundred home runs.

~

So what was it like to pitch to Joe DiMaggio?
Mel Parnell:

I knew I had a battle on my hands, because the guy was a great hitter. Looking in at him at the plate, I knew I had to be careful with each and every pitch. I tried to pitch him inside. Mainly to keep his elbows close into his body so he couldn't get his arms extended. If he got his arms extended, of course, that's where power lies.

He had a great eye and great knowledge where the strike zone was. You don't see too much of that. You see some of these guys swinging at balls on the outside; they can't stop the bat. He didn't do that.

A baseball player's prime years are generally between the ages of twenty-eight and thirty-two. DiMaggio joined the service when he was twenty-eight and returned to the Yankees when he was thirty-one.

And he was aging quickly. In the course of his career, he suffered through a range of ailments: knee problems, bone chips in his throwing arm, bone spurs in his heels, an aching back, an eye infection, sore shoulders, sore ankles.

I REMEMBER JOE DIMAGGIO

It was getting harder and harder to be the Great DiMaggio. But some of his finest performances emerged from the pain.

DiMaggio missed the first two months of the 1949 season with an agonizing bone spur in his heel. On June 28, the Yankees visited Fenway Park for a three-game series against the powerful Red Sox, who were beginning to pull away from New York in the pennant chase.

Dick Caime *was a Yankee fan in Brooklyn at the time. He recalls the importance of the healthy return of Joe D.:*

There was one particular series against the Red Sox in Fenway when Joe D. was coming off the bone-spur heel operation when I prayed on hands and knees for his comeback and success. My friends, mostly Dodger fans, laughed at me.

So when I went to confession that Saturday (we would go even with nothing to confess, especially if we had nothing to confess), I told the priest what I was praying for. He smiled that Bing Crosby-Barry Fitzgerald Irish smile and said, "Can't you think of something more important to pray for?" and I said, "Like what?"

His laughter shook the whole church, Saint Brigid. I was embarrassed to go out of the confessional.[9]

$\sim$

The Great DiMaggio returned. In the three games, he hit four home runs and drove in nine runs. The Yankees swept.

84

THE GREAT DiMAGGIO

Before the third game, a group of Yankees gathered around the batting cage to watch Ted Williams hit.

"Why don't you fellows get away from there," snapped Yankee coach Frank Crosetti, "and come into the dugout and admire DiMaggio?"

"Guess you're right," said Yankee manager Casey Stengel, and he headed to the dugout.[10]

Mel Parnell *was the Red Sox starter in the third game:*

He had a home run in each of the first two games we played. I made the statement before the game, "Hell, he's not going to get a home run off of me, even if I have to walk him four times." It just so happens in the game, I got him out the first three times up. We're leading in the ball game and he comes up with two men on base. I'm getting smart. I figure my fastball is my best pitch on that particular day. I figured if he's going to beat me, he's going to have to beat me with my fastball.

So I threw a fastball to him and he hits a big, high foul ball outside of first base. Billy Goodman, who was playing first base, goes over to the coaching box to try to make the play and he drops the ball. So I'm starting to think a little bit more. I'm thinking I got the fastball past him, because he fouled it to the opposite side of the field. So I threw him another fastball and he hits a little squibbler around home plate that goes foul. So this is making me even smarter.

So I throw him another fastball and he hits the damn thing up in the light tower and wins the ball game. I'll never forget that one.

Neither would DiMaggio. At the end of his career, he called the fifty-six-game hitting streak his top baseball thrill. Second was his comeback outburst in Boston.
  Jerry Coleman:

He was happy as a clam. We're on the train, and he's sitting at one of the tables. He said, "Can't beat this life, kid." That was his way of showing happiness. That was his whole life.

*Red Sox right-hander **Boo Ferriss**:*

He tore us up. He murdered us. He came back and, oh man, it was like he'd never been away. We couldn't get him out.

Still, by the outbreak of the Korean War, he was the Pretty Good DiMaggio.
  *Teammate **Bobby Brown**:*

He was in terrible pain. He had a lot of trouble with his back. I know that after games that last year, year and a half, he'd go home and sit in a hot bathtub for several hours. He was just hurting.

It was funny. He never lost any of his speed. He could still run. But he didn't throw as well. And he wasn't quite the devastating hitter that he had been. I think the slider on the outside part of the plate was beginning to bother him.

Jerry Coleman:

After World War II, it wasn't the same DiMaggio, because he just lost three years that he couldn't replace. His hitting wasn't as good.

He was hurting at the end. He couldn't pull the ball. He got a lot of hits in '50 to keep his average, but they were the other way. That part of his life was gone. He couldn't get that bat around the way he used to when he was younger. And his last year, he got a lot of hits to right field.

Former Philadelphia Athletics shortstop **Eddie Joost**:

The last couple of years, you could see there was something wrong. He had a bone spur taken out of his heel. That really bothered him continuously. He was in pain.

You could tell that. The way he went after a ball. He wouldn't get there. Before, he'd be standing there.

The operation on his heel slowed him down a full step. If you saw him running the bases after that, you could see him limping. Not considerably. But you could see he was a little tender running on that foot that was operated on.

~

Celtics legend **Red Auerbach** *remembers the long-term effects of DiMaggio's playing days:*

He was a good friend of Sid Luckman, for years. He and I and Sid went to make an appearance in Hershey, Pennsylvania. Joe said to me, "A lot of people think it was my heels that were bothering me, the spurs. It was my back. The whole thing was my back." He kept telling me that.

About eight, ten years ago, he came down to Washington for an Old Timers game. I was sitting with Joe out on the dugout. He was saying, "Geez, my back is killing me." But as soon as they called his name, he shook it off and he trotted out. He must have been in a hell of a lot of pain.

~

THE GREAT DiMAGGIO

Casey Stengel, in 1950:

Is he through? Ha! I'd like to have a dozen washed-up ballplayers like him.[11]

~

He was aging and he was hurting, which brought small indignities to the most dignified DiMaggio.

Casey Stengel, whose fun-loving, almost clownish approach to managing left DiMaggio unamused, experimented by dropping him to fifth in the batting order.

Coleman:

This is where he and Stengel separated. Joe hit fourth his whole life. And he came into the clubhouse and saw he was in the fifth position. I don't think he ever forgave Stengel for that. Now, that's just my summation. But I think there was definitely a cooling.

~

He agonized to keep his batting average above .300.

Coleman *remembers a comical moment during DiMaggio's quest, while also remembering that DiMaggio never meant to be comical on the ball field:*

The '50 season, and we're going down to the wire, and Joe's hitting .29999 or something, and he wants the

.300. We're playing in Philadelphia. He hit a rocket to Eddie Joost and he was out.

On the way out to center field, he was mumbling to himself—he didn't say much, but he was a mumbler now and then—and Yogi airmailed a ball over my head, you know, when the catcher throws the ball down to second base when they're throwing it around. And it hit DiMaggio in the heel! And down he went. I turn around and he's looking at me. He thinks I did it. He says, "God——it," and he threw the ball and it bounced in front of me and hits me in the knee.

And now I'm down. We're both rolling around on the ground.

Stengel even tried DiMaggio, the greatest center fielder of his generation, at first base, traditionally the last stop for broken-down outfielders and catchers.

Coleman:

One day in Washington, and I know Casey discussed it with him, Casey wanted him to play first base. I almost got him killed.

We had a triple play in the offing. Runners at first and second and a line shot to Rizzuto. I went over and got the guy at second and threw the ball to first. The guy between first and second, instead of sliding, hunched up. The ball hit his shoulder and Joe was in a spread-out position with his glove up there and the ball went by his face by about two inches. I could see the headlines: "Coleman Fired for Killing DiMaggio."

He was only at first base for one game.

~

There was only one way for the Great DiMaggio to deal with the loss of his skills. He hinted at it on the last day of the 1949 season, in the pennant-deciding game against the Red Sox.

Weakened by illness, he failed to reach a catchable fly ball hit by Bobby Doerr. The ball fell for a triple, prolonging a Boston rally.

Coleman:

Doerr hit a ball to straightaway center field. He didn't get it. He knew he should have. He took himself out of the game. It was that simple.

Joe could go to the wall and catch anything. But the ball got over his head. He was sick—the day before, they had a day for him and he had the flu. He looked awful. He was probably about ten pounds under, maybe more.

Consequently, when that play happened, he just left the field. He knew he should have had it. Nobody said a word. We all knew it.

~

Betty Glick *was a teenager in Erie, Pennsylvania, in the 1930s. She remembers a longtime desire to see the Great*

I REMEMBER JOE DIMAGGIO

DiMaggio play, and finally feeling like many twentieth-century baseball fans—like she had missed something:

I was a Yankee fan. On my wall were pictures of Lou Gehrig, Joe DiMaggio, and Tyrone Power.

Erie was near Cleveland, but I didn't particularly like the Cleveland teams. Whenever the Yankees played Cleveland, I was able to hear them on the radio. That's the only thing I read in the sports pages. I didn't know a thing about any other sport. I had two cousins who lived in New York. One was a Dodger fan and one was a Giants fan. When I'd go to New York, they wouldn't take me to Yankee Stadium. I had to either go to the Polo Grounds or to Ebbets Field. I desperately wanted to see Joe DiMaggio play.

So when my husband graduated from the University of Wisconsin and we moved to New York—his first job was in New York—the first thing we did was pack up our little kid, who was about five or six at the time, and we were off to Yankee Stadium.

First on my agenda was getting to Yankee Stadium, because I wanted to see Joe DiMaggio. We were as poor as church mice, and we even had to scrape the bottom of the barrel for the three of us to go to Yankee Stadium. We lived in Brooklyn, so we had to take the subway to the Bronx. Being new in New York, it was really an adventure. I was just overjoyed.

We got there early and we saw them warm up. I was so excited. And that was the day he played one inning, and they took him out and put in some young punk named Mickey Mantle. I was so angry and so disappointed. I just saw that one inning of Joe DiMaggio.

We stayed and watched the game. But I muttered through the whole thing.

DiMaggio was a master of his craft. Hall of Famer **Monte Irvin***:*

I came up as an outfielder, and I wanted to learn how to play center field. So I went to Yankee Stadium and watched Joe. When a ball is hit straight over your head, what is the first move you make? I watched Joe. If I got in a slump at bat, I watched Joe. He'd stand there flat-footed with the bat cocked, probably didn't stride more than six inches. If the pitcher threw a fastball, he'd come around swiftly with that bat. If it was a change of pace, then, because he didn't stride much, he could still hit it 420 feet.

DiMaggio batted only .263 with twelve home runs in his final season. But his contribution always exceeded the numbers. **Phil Rizzuto***, in the summer of '51:*

Things ain't going so good with the club and you can't buy a win for love or money and you feel low. Then you look up and see the big guy, standing there. So you feel everything is okay. Even if he doesn't hit so good and he doesn't field like he used to, he just makes the rest of the club feel that they're Yankees. He's as much the inspiration for the club as the uniform.[13]

⌐⌐

Following the 1951 season, DiMaggio and a group of major- and minor-leaguers toured Japan. They played in front of large, appreciative crowds.

In Tokyo, Joe DiMaggio played his last competitive baseball game.

Brother **Dominic DiMaggio** *was also on the trip:*

It was his last at-bat. He wanted to go out with distinction. They kept changing pitchers every few innings. I hit before him and he came to me and he wanted to know, "What's this guy doing? What's he throwing?" I told him that I had him 3-0 and 3-1 and he threw me a screwball each time. Joe said, "Okay."

He got up and I think it was 2-0 and he threw him a screwball and he hit it into the seats, into the bleachers.

He came back into the dugout and said, "That's it, gentlemen. That's my farewell. I'm not playing tomorrow."

⌐⌐

Pirates outfielder **Dino Restelli** *was on the Japan tour:*

He hung around with Lefty O'Doul a lot. They were kind of buddy-buddy. He had played ball for O'Doul in the thirties. So there was a good association there. I remember coming down for breakfast one morning and seeing them sitting together. So I walked by and Joe said, "Come on, sit down and have a cup of coffee with us." He was always very friendly to me.

He and Lefty O'Doul used to come out to the ball-park after we all took our batting practice. The game was at one o'clock and they would show up at five minutes till one. They were with all the celebrities. Even the Emperor had him in for a visit. DiMaggio was the biggest thing, along with Lefty O'Doul.

He didn't play many games. And when he did play, he would play maybe four or five innings. He wouldn't play the whole ball game. At the time, he was having a problem. He was always saying something like, "God, my feet hurt. My back hurts. My hip hurts." And he said to all of us who were sitting around, "You know, when baseball ceases to be fun, you know it's time to quit."

⌒

Casey Stengel:

He was our silent leader. Without him we couldn't have won the pennant last season. He always gave everything he had, no matter how badly he felt. He served as an inspiration to the rest of the club. He was more than just a player. He was an institution.[12]

⌒

His body broke, but his approach to playing baseball was the same every time he picked up a bat or ball.

Mel Parnell:

The last year we had a ball club down here in New Orleans, the Pelicans, I managed the ball club. We were in spring training. It was probably around 1960.

Joe came to town, and I got him out to the ballpark and he was watching the practices and everything. And, of course, they wanted to see Joe swing the bat. So I said, "Hey, Joe, how about getting up there and taking a few strokes?" He did. He was dressed up in a suit, with a necktie and everything. He got up and he hit one out of the ballpark. *He was wearing a suit.* Of course, that's all the fans wanted to see.

HIS WAY

"If he said hello to you, that was a long conversation."

—HANK GREENBERG

No one could really figure him out. Biographers, teammates, opponents, cronies, wives, his son, baseball writers, fans, and autograph seekers tried and tried, but could really only agree on one thing.

He was private, quiet, and tough to figure out. His pal, the famous New York sportswriter Jimmy Cannon, said he didn't know him well, although he killed a lot of time in his company.

Something else was obvious: To be Joe DiMaggio, and pull all that attention and adoration and favoritism and groveling and devotion, must have been wonderful—and horrible.

DiMaggio was genuinely shy, and there is evidence that he wished he could be more outgoing. He just couldn't. He probably also enjoyed watching everyone try to solve the mystery. Why should he solve it for them? Most people followed his baseball career over the radio and used their imaginations to draw a picture of him as a player. They might as well use their imaginations to draw a picture of him as a person. It wasn't a bad policy. Almost everyone wanted to adore him—he was their boyhood hero, or their dad's boyhood hero—so they were generous when filling in the blanks.

The truth is, he was a major celebrity for seven decades, so there is anecdotal evidence to support a sweeping range of views of him. He was moody, gracious, cheap, generous, aloof, attentive, rude, kind, difficult, helpful, shy, happy to sign autographs, nasty about signing autographs, charming, boring, pleasant, and impatient. Depending on whom you ask.

A walk, then, through the years for various impressions of Joe DiMaggio:

⌒

Dario Lodigiani remembers a young pal from the Great Depression days in San Francisco:

One thing about Joe, he liked to sleep. With the San Francisco Boys Club, we played semipro baseball. If you didn't go get him, he'd stay in bed. We always said, "Joe, with the way he sleeps, he'll never get in trouble."

Joe went to Galileo High School, and he was there a coupla months, and he dropped out. He never went to school anymore. Dominic was a year behind me. Dominic DiMaggio was the only one in his family to graduate high school. I wouldn't say his studies came hard to Joe. He just didn't care about them. If Joe made a point to actually learn something, he would have been a good student. Joe, he was pretty sharp. He knew how to handle all those people when he got to the big leagues. The education he got there, you couldn't get in college.

Joe, when he got to the Yankees, and then he came home, he was so in demand. Somebody was always asking him to come here or go there. His life changed a lot. Everybody wanted to be around Joe DiMaggio. He was graceful and he did a lot of those things, especially if it was for charity. They made such a big fuss over him when he got home. After he played a few years in the big leagues, you could tell there was a change in his life.

⁓

Steve Barath *remembers the young DiMaggio:*

I was his roommate for two years. I played third base. In '34 and '35. With the San Francisco Seals.

Some sportswriters came up to our room in Sacramento once. Sportswriters came up and asked Joe who was his roommate. And he pointed at my suitcase. He said, "That's my roommate. He hardly ever comes in early enough for me to see him. He's always out dancing."

I Remember Joe DiMaggio

Joe was never friendly. I mean, he was friendly with me, but he didn't want to go out. He was just scared of the world. Shy. That's the word for him.

⌒

Yankee pitcher **Lefty Gomez** *remembers a Yankees team-mate, five years his junior and dealing with fame:*

Everybody who knew Joe in those days knew he didn't talk. I remember a two-week road trip—New York, Chicago, Detroit, Cleveland, and Saint Louis. Two weeks, not one word. I'll tell you what he did do. He would take along one of those small radios and listen to the radio, the big band music and those old quiz shows, Dr. I.Q. and things like that. He'd read the sports pages and he'd read . . . Superman comics.

One day we were walking down the street of some town and he suddenly turns to me and says, "Lefty, you know what day today is?" I say, "Yeah, Wednesday." Then he says, "No, no, today is the day the new Superman comes out." Every Wednesday there was a new issue. So now he sees this newspaper stand and looks to see if they got comic books. He points to it and wants me to get it for him. He stands off to the side. Hell, he was Joe DiMaggio and if the newsstand guy saw him buy Superman comics it would be all over the world. I got one of those faces nobody could ever recognize so he wants me to buy it for him.

"Joe, is this what you want, the Superman comics?"

He looks around at a couple of people there and he says, "No, you know I wouldn't buy that." Then I walk away, and he motions again. I finally buy it for him and he stuffs it into his pocket. He spends the night with Superman.[1]

~

*Yankees outfielder **Tommy Henrich** remembers the shy, prewar DiMaggio speaking up:*

Hank Greenberg, with the Tigers, he hit our pitching pretty well. He was a very valuable guy for their ball club. He was very respected. I think he would bear down against the Yankees because he didn't sign up to be a Yankee because of Gehrig being there. He was no dummy.

Anyway, we're bringing in Murphy again, this time in Detroit. The bullpen was straight back of the center fielder. Walking in, he has to pass Joe DiMaggio in cen-ter field. And as he goes by, Joe DiMaggio said, "Why don't we fastball this guy for once?" Because we would curve him to try to get him out—curve him, curve him, curve him.

It was very, very strange for DiMaggio. It was a real odd thing. He didn't give advice to anybody.

So Murphy passes by. He mulls this thing over. He says, "Maybe that's a doggone good idea. Fool him a lit-tle bit." So Johnny threw the first pitch. Fastball.

Boom. Downtown. Greenberg beats us again.

Game's over. We're in the clubhouse. We're down. Nobody's saying *boo*. After three or four minutes, we were in there sitting down. DiMaggio is sitting about ten feet across from me and about fifteen feet up from me is Murphy.

DiMaggio stood up and went to Johnny Murphy and he said, "I want to tell you something. Don't you ever listen to another doggone word that I ever say." And he walked back.

That was a long speech for Joe.

Lee Stine, a former Seals teammate, recalls joining with him again in the major leagues:

I went to the Yankees in '38 when Joe was there. Cincinnati had sent me over there. After he held out, I remember I walked into the clubhouse in Yankee Stadium. Joe was there. First thing he did was jump out of his seat, off of his stool there in front of his locker, and run over to me. "Lee! Lee! How are you?" See, I hadn't seen him since 1933. He treated me like I was his long-lost cousin or something. The other players, the Yankees, were looking over as if to say, "Who's that? Why is Joe making such a fuss over him?"

Joe and I were real close. He and I and Lefty Gomez would do a lot of things together. We would go to the theater and things like that. We'd be sitting in the lobby, and Joe would be there, and Gomez would say,

"Come on, come on, we're going to the show." We'd try to sit in the balcony someplace, way off. On the side or something. The three of us were always together, although they were great players, and I wasn't. Gomez was talking, talking, talking, all the time. He and Joe were different personalities, altogether. He was a funny guy, too, Gomez. But they were very good friends.

Joe was the kind of guy who it might be hard to write a spectacular story about. He was just an ordinary person. That's just the way he was naturally. That's the way he was born. He didn't want to put on any phony-baloney stuff. He had a brother, Vince, who did a lot of talking. Popping off. They were completely opposite.

He was quiet. That was his way of life, no matter where he was. He was quiet and he minded his own business. Got along with everybody. He didn't put up any phony pretense of anything with anybody. He treated everybody the same. I liked Joe very much. Don't get me wrong. He was a great guy. But how are you going to write a story about a guy who sits in the lobby and reads the paper, then goes up to his room and takes a nap?

Phil Rizzuto remembers seeing Joe DiMaggio's leadership style at spring training, when the Scooter was a rookie:

The way they would work it, they had the eight regulars of the previous year take hitting practice. Joe McCarthy had said to me, "Now Phil, you hit at batting practice with the regulars." So I was supposed to be hitting in the number-nine spot. Well, it seemed like after the eighth man hit, the first man would jump back in and of course, being a rookie, I couldn't say, well, It's my turn. And they just wouldn't let me in there at bat.

DiMaggio saw what was going on immediately but didn't say anything until his third day in camp. That morning, after the eighth man in the lineup had hit and the number-one man was about to jump back into the batting cage, DiMaggio, standing close by, hollered, "Rizzuto, come on; get in there and hit. We want to see what you can do."

That's how DiMaggio was a leader. Joe didn't go to the other guys and say, "Let this kid hit." He just did it by indirection, by example. After that, he began to help me out a little and he sort of broke the ice. And so when the other fellows saw Joe do that, then little by little they came over and started to joke with me, and from then on, it was more relaxing.[2]

~

Johnny Sturm *was a rookie first baseman on the 1941* *Yankees:*

Joe was kind of a stranger, to almost everybody. He was a helluva nice guy, as far as I knew. I knew his whole family. I played with Vince and I played with Dom. They always used to tell me that their oldest brother was the best ballplayer. That was Tom. All three of them said Tom was always the best ballplayer. But he had to stay home and work.

Joe and Gomez used to room together on the road. Gomez was always comical. You've got one guy who was a comedian, and one guy who was just as straight-faced as can be. Gomez was always in good spirits all the time. That was a good thing for Joe. He kept Joe bouncing a little bit.

As time went on, there was a reversal. DiMaggio was good for Gomez. At that time, Gomez was getting older. We had two rookie pitchers on the team. I think they won twenty or twenty-one ball games in Double-A the year before. They were kind of looking for a starting job. Every time Gomez would pitch, why, you could bet that the Dago was really on his toes. Joe always had a good day when Gomez was pitching. That really helped Gomez out. Gomez and Joe were always good buddies.

You run into a guy like Joe. If you're not around him a lot, you wouldn't pick up the little things about him. He didn't do much. Joe and I talked all the time. About everything. About Vince, his brother, and where I played with him. His family. We talked about fishing and things like that. We talked about the restaurant business. Tom DiMaggio had opened up the restaurant in San Francisco. Joe would have to go there and help out a little bit in the wintertime. He had to be kind of a host. You know—trying to work up the business. He didn't like that. He didn't like that at all. People looking at him. He didn't care for that at all.

We were invited up to his place one time. But it got too late, and we said, "No, we got to go on home." He had an apartment there in New York. It was about eleven o'clock. We just said, "We should go on home. Joe will probably be going to bed, too."

You know, Joe actually had two different lives. One as a ballplayer and a social life. And not too many ballplayers got into that social life at all.

Gomez wouldn't have said too much. He was talkative, but not about Joe. Those guys, they would quiet up in a hurry. In their social life, if you wanted to know anything about Joe, you couldn't find out much about that. They'd all clam right up. You know, because Joe was in that Hollywood crowd. That show crowd. That fast crowd. Especially out there on the coast. He'd get in with that fast track out there. He got in there with them boys. Frenchy Bordagaray used to tell Joe, "Joe, you better be careful of that crowd." Because Frenchy was in the show business. He used to tell Joe, "You be careful about them." That part of Joe would be a different story completely than the baseball story.

I ran into him in the Meulebach Hotel in Kansas City one morning. I was managing the Joplin ball club. This was in 1949, I think. The Yankees were playing in Kansas City. They must have been playing an exhibition game or something. We were staying at the Meulebach. I came down to breakfast and there was old Joe. He was reading the paper there. He said, "Hey, John. Is this you here in the paper? I'm looking at your average here in the paper. I see you're hitting .425. You mean to tell me you're hitting .425 with them bad lights and everything else? Come on and sit down and have breakfast with me." So we had breakfast together. We talked things over.

⌒

*Yankees relief pitcher **Johnny Murphy** remembers going to the movies with a gang of teammates one evening:*

We sat up in the balcony. We were in the front part and I happened to look around and in the very last row of the balcony I see Joe DiMaggio, all alone . . . I walked up to him. He said, "Well, I knew somebody who got me in through the back elevator. It left me right off behind the balcony. I just stayed here in the last row to see the movie. It's the only place I have peace and quiet . . ."

It must have been tough for him. He could never go anywhere in public like the rest of us without being bothered. He just couldn't drop into a restaurant; he'd be swamped, they'd tear off his clothes. The autograph seekers would annoy him so much that it took all the fun out of going anywhere.[3]

⌒

Jack Mahon, *a reporter for the International News Service, remembers hanging around the lobby of the Chase Hotel in Saint Louis one lazy day in the thirties. Tony Lazzeri, Frankie Crosetti, and DiMaggio were hanging around, too:*

I bought a paper and sat down near them and after a while became aware of the fact that none of them had a word to say to the others. Just for fun I timed them to see how long they would maintain their silence. Believe it or not, they didn't speak for an hour and twenty minutes. At the end of the time DiMaggio cleared his throat. Crosetti looked at him and said: "What did you say?" And Lazzeri said, "Shut up. He didn't say nothing." They lapsed into silence and at the end of ten more minutes I got up and left. I couldn't stand it anymore.

Minor-leaguer **Chuck Stevens** *remembers Sergeant DiMaggio of the United States Army Air Corps during World War II:*

We played a fundraising game against the Santa Ana air station. Joe was on that ball club. Red Ruffing introduced me to Joe. I remember that at that time, Joe was going through a divorce. That was discussed. Three or four of us sat around and talked about things in general. Being in the service, that sort of thing. I immediately liked him. He was quiet, dignified.

A divorce has to be the toughest thing that could happen. And he handled that with a great deal of dignity. There isn't anybody who can go through a divorce without it having a tremendous emotional impact on you. I'm sure it did on Joe. But he didn't publicly make any noise about it. I was very impressed with that.

Here's a scene that is certainly from a bygone era—photographers right on top of the action. This is DiMaggio at bat early in the 1938 season. (AP/Wide World Photos)

⌒

*Yankees teammate **Jerry Coleman** remembers the Great DiMaggio's clubhouse presence after the war:*

He was not a talker. His conversations were, "Hrrrrr-arrrrr-errr." In the clubhouse, he'd sit in his locker, which was six or seven removed from mine, and he'd say, "HalfcupcoffPete." If you wanted to translate that, it was "Half a cup of coffee, Pete." If you didn't know what he wanted, you had no idea what he said.

⌒

*Yankees teammate **Bobby Brown**:*

He wasn't a guy who talked much or rotated around the clubhouse making small talk. He kept to himself. And if you wanted to talk to him, fine. He was very cordial. But he was not someone who initiated a lot of conversation. He would say something during the ball game to you, if it was meaningful. But basically, he was a very quiet, introverted guy. He bothered no one and no one bothered him.

⌒

Dario Lodigiani *remembers coming to New York with the White Sox and visiting his boyhood chum:*

He invited me when we were in New York to come up to his apartment. We'd have a beer or two, then go out and have dinner somewhere. I'd do the same for him in Chicago. The poor guy, it was tough on him. Joe would start a parade when he went anywhere. Right away, he attracted attention. I know that room service was a big thing with Joe.

He'd call someplace and we'd go in a corner to eat. Because he couldn't eat. Everybody would be bothering him. He got to be a big man in New York.

~

Bill Raimondi *remembers bumping into DiMaggio nearly two decades after they played against one another in the Pacific Coast League:*

When he came out with the Yankees in 1951, I was with Los Angeles. He asked to see me.

We must have talked for a half-hour on the first-base line. That was the first time I ever saw him talk that long to anybody. It made me feel kind of honored.

~

I Remember Joe DiMaggio

Robert J. S. Ross, of Worcester, Massachusetts:

To us kids who lived around Yankee Stadium in the 1950s, Joe DiMaggio's reputation as the best player ever was not as important as his aloofness.

When we clustered at the players' entrance, Phil Rizzuto lined us up and signed every autograph request. Whitey Ford smiled and made a pass at signing, too. Billy Martin was excited by our attention, and Mel Allen actually talked to us.

DiMaggio once started his car with my young arms inside it, grubby pad of paper still extended to him, and I was bruised in more ways than one. Maybe it had to do with center fielders: Mickey Mantle, another center fielder, once kicked me. I know that locals see things differently from tourists, but although I still admire Joe DiMaggio, I've never completely forgiven him.[4]

*Yankees backup catcher **Charlie Silvera** remembers DiMaggio, the big star desperately seeking small pleasures:*

He was a regular guy. He loved to sit down and talk with the guys. But he couldn't be with us anywhere. People bothered him. I remember we were in a movie theater in Seattle and the lights came up, and everybody noticed Joe. He couldn't eat by himself. If he ate with us, we'd have to shoo people away. People recognized him. You could have a hundred thousand people out on a field and you could look and say, "There's Joe." He had that distinct look about him.

He was quiet. He didn't volunteer a lot of information. Many times after games at Yankee Stadium, he'd come over and have a couple of beers and just talked baseball. Two hours after the game, or maybe three, we'd all get dressed and go outside to catch a cab, and people would still be waiting for him. Finally, they had to sneak him out through center field, where the cab would wait there for him.

He was always great to me and my wife. Especially after I got to the Yankees. He would always give us tickets to stage shows through his friends. That's how I got to meet Marilyn. She was sitting with Joe behind us at intermission. I almost fell out of my seat.

I was left behind in Saint Petersburg once because he had the spur in his heel. They left two pitchers and myself to catch batting practice. We stayed there for about ten days while the club played their way north. Joe would always have a case of beer for us after the workout.

I got to know him a little on the train. He didn't play cards. He'd sleep. We always said he could fall asleep on a meat hook. He would fall asleep sitting up. We'd be going from Boston to New York, and he'd sleep. He relaxed.

He always talked about people wanting to make a movie. He said, "I'm not going to give anybody my life history. I'll do it up good when the time comes." And he never did. Like writing a book. He never did that, either.

113

I REMEMBER JOE DIMAGGIO

Saloonkeeper **Toots Shor** *remembers DiMaggio finding the gift of privacy in his Manhattan gin mill:*

If the Yankees had won, he would come into the place and sit at his regular table and I'd eat with him. Nobody bothered him. Everybody would look at him, but nobody would bother him. In our joint if a guy wants to give autographs, fine; but if he doesn't, we don't let the customers bother him. All the waiters knew how to handle that. If the Yankees won and he had a good day and was feeling all right physically—Joe was hurt a lot because he played so hard—some of the sportswriters would come over. He never pushed himself on them. They would just come over . . .

    Joe would sit there. He wouldn't say much, just listen to those lies. He loved Looie Effrat from the *Times*. Looie made him laugh a lot, and Jimmy Cannon was probably his closest friend—they would spend a lot of time together. He admired Bill Corum and Granny Rice and Arthur Daley and Red Smith. He used to love to sit and listen to Red talk. He never had to be afraid of those guys: They would never write anything he told them in the joint. He knew they were off duty and he was off duty.[5]

Red Sox infielder **Johnny Pesky** *remembers two sides of his Yankee opponent:*

He was kind of a stone-faced guy. He didn't smile much when he was playing. I asked the clubhouse kids once what kind of guy DiMaggio was. They said he was very quiet. He'd sit in front of his locker and have two or three cups of coffee. Black coffee.

But he'd kid with me a little bit. This was back in the years when we left the gloves on the field. He chewed gum. He'd come by me and he'd wad up a piece of gum and he'd hit me with it. He'd say, "Here you go, clubhouse kid."

Red Sox pitcher **Mel Parnell** *remembers breaking through with DiMaggio far away from Yankee Stadium and Fenway Park:*

We were on a tour of Japan together in 1951. I really got to know him. I thought he was a great person. He was a quiet, timid fellow. You had to joke around and get him loosened up. And when you got him loosened up, boy, he was just enjoyable. He was the kind of guy who you get a drink into him and he'd get talkative. Just a great guy.

I've heard a lot of people say they didn't like him because he wasn't too talkative. He was shy. But if you got a drink in him and got him started in conversation, you'd love the guy.

The Italian-American Association wanted to have him down here to New Orleans for a banquet. They asked me if I'd call him. So I called him in San Francisco and Joe came down for it. And the guys didn't like him too much. They said, "Man, he's too quiet. He didn't want to talk." And I said, "Well, Joe's a very quiet guy, a very timid person."

So later, the same group had a golf tournament down here and they wanted to get him back. I said, "Look, you guys, when you get him back, put a drink or two in him and get the guy talking, you're going to love him." They did that and they said, "Oh, what a great guy he is." A complete opposite of their first opinion of him. Joe was that way.

⌒

Yankees infielder **Bobby Brown** *was serving as an army doctor in Japan in 1954 when newlyweds DiMaggio and Marilyn Monroe visited. Brown remembers the solicitous groom:*

He was a little skeptical of the army, having served in the army in World War II. Marilyn was going to go to Korea to entertain the troops. She was going to need some injections, for cholera and yellow fever and typhoid and so forth.

He came out with the announcement that no army doctor would have anything to do with Mrs. DiMaggio except First Lieutenant Brown. So of course, from all over the Far East, came the calls, "Who the hell is First Lieutenant Brown?" He just didn't want anybody who he didn't know dealing with her.

HIS WAY

Patricia Donnelly Harris, Miss America 1939 and wife
of Hearst newspaperman Robin Harris, remembers
DiMaggio on the town in the fifties:

Georgie Solotaire was a mutual friend. He was one of
our best friends. Georgie was a funny little man, a tiny
little man, about five-four, five-five. He was a ticket
broker. Joe, after he left Marilyn, Georgie moved in
with him. They lived at the Madison Hotel. We used to
meet Joe and George at a restaurant on the East Side
called Christ Cella's.

Everybody was hanging around Toots Shor's. Toots
used to give a lot of private parties upstairs. No one ever
bothered anybody at Toots'. Gleason was there. He'd
get so drunk that he'd fall asleep right in the entrance
to the dining room. Toots would say, "Leave him alone,"
and everybody would step over him. All of the stars
were there. It was a great place because it was private.
No one bothered anybody.

We were there one night. I was standing at the bar
getting a drink. Joe came in with Marilyn. He came up
to me and introduced her. We stood and talked for a few
minutes. None of us were very outgoing. We were all
very quiet. So we didn't have an awful lot to say.

She seemed to be quite shy. She seemed to be rather
quiet, not too sure of herself. I said, "Can I get you a
drink? Would you like a drink?" She said, "Oh, no. I
don't drink." Later in the evening I saw her having a
great time drinking.

Joe was a very private person. We had dinner quite a few times after he and Marilyn broke up. No one ever thought to ask questions. You just didn't invade his privacy. He was just standoffish. Private. He wasn't snooty in any sense. But he was very definitely private.

⌒

New York criminal lawyer and baseball author **Doug Lyons**:

My father's name was Leonard Lyons. He was a syndicated columnist for the *New York Post* for forty years. He knew everybody in New York—athletes, writers, artists, filmmakers, everybody who was worth knowing, he knew them. One year in the same mail, we got a Christmas card from J. Edgar Hoover and Lucky Luciano.

DiMaggio's best friend in New York was a press agent named George Solotaire. My father told a story that he and Solotaire and Joe and Marilyn are out for dinner.

And Solotaire closes his eyes for a while. He said, "I thought they wanted to be alone."

⌒

New York City policeman **Everett Parker**:

There was a bachelor party, he was a friend of mine, who was a sergeant. Fifty years old and he got married. The bachelor party was held in Toots Shor's. Before the main event, the bachelor party, I got there with three other guys who worked the Manhattan Precinct. We went to the bar, a circular bar that Toots Shor had. On the other side of the bar was Toots Shor himself, Horace McMahon—he was the actor in *The Naked City*. He played Lieutenant Parker. And Joe D., sitting in the middle of those. So you had Toots, you had Joe, and you had a Hollywood actor.

They took us for cops. They could see we were cops. We had a drink and the bartender brought us a second, "Compliments of Mr. McMahon." So Horace bought a drink. But Joe and Toots Shor just smiled. Maybe he did have, as I later heard about Joe D., that he had short arms and long pockets. We got a smile out of him, but we never got a drink.

⌒

Danny Onisko remembers meeting the retired DiMaggio, who was working for a company that supplied food to American military bases around the world:

It was the summer of '59. I was eleven. My dad was in the air force and we were stationed on Guam. I worked at the youth center on base. One morning when I went to work, my boss, who was a sergeant, said, "Hey, go get a baseball." I said, "A hardball or a softball?" He said, "A hardball." So I went to a storage room and got a baseball in a box all wrapped up in white tissue paper and gave it to him. He took it out of the box and gave it to me. I looked at him kind of blank, like "What's this for?" and he said, "Just hang on to that."

About twenty minutes later, this big, tall guy comes in. Joe DiMaggio. I didn't know who he was at the time. The sergeant was standing there at the door. He was expecting him. I was just kind of standing in the sergeant's shadow. Joe DiMaggio came in and shook his hand. They talked like they were old-time buddies. Joe DiMaggio saw that I had this baseball and he said, "Do you want me to autograph that?" I looked at him as if to say, "What?" The sergeant started shaking his head yes. And Joe DiMaggio took the ball and he signed it, and he gave it back to me.

The sergeant said, "Danny here is my right-hand guy. He'll show you around the youth center." He introduced me to him, Joe DiMaggio, which still didn't mean a thing to me. We walked around the youth center, and I showed him where the big kids had a poolroom and all that. He was very friendly. It was like we were the only two people in the room. He was totally focused on me.

He asked me if I played baseball. I said, yeah, and he asked me what position. I told him they had me playing everywhere, in the outfield, first base. He asked me, "Well, what do you really like?" I said, "Well, I really kind of like being out in the field catching fly balls." He said, "Yeah, I've seen a few fly balls." He looked at me with this big smile. He had big teeth.

We walked back to the sergeant's office. He had stopped at Guam to refuel his airplane. He was on his way to Japan for an exhibition baseball game. He thanked me for showing him around, told me to hang on to that ball.

I went home for lunch and said, "Hey, Mom. Look what I got. I got an autographed ball from Joe . . ." And I couldn't even remember his last name. My mom made a big deal. She said, "That's Joe DiMaggio." Then my dad came home for lunch from working on the flight line. He started telling Mom they were refueling Joe DiMaggio's plane. She tells him about the ball. Of course, he gets all excited. He asked me if it would be okay if he took the ball down to the flight line to show the guys. Which he did. I'm thinking, *Wow, I've really got something here. I don't know what it is, but I'm going to find out.*

I had a marble bag. It was a purple velvet bag that whiskey came in. Royal Crown. I dumped my marbles out and put my ball in this bag. And that's where it's been for forty years. I've shown it to everybody I've known.

What it's meant to me is, that there was an adult who took the time to give a kid some contact. My dad was never home, being in the military. It just meant a lot to me that this guy, this big, giant-like guy, towering above me, took the time to get into my world and say hello.

I still think about it. We were getting Christmas stuff out the other day. The baseball is stored with our Christmas stuff, so it would be in a safe spot. We came across it. We sat there in the shed, looking at it and talking about it, my son and I. He knows the story. He's heard it all his life. It moves me when I think about it. When he (Joe) died, it was like a part of me died. It was like losing a family member.

I REMEMBER JOE DIMAGGIO

Frank Gifford, *New York football Giants star, was a*
fledgling WCBS radio sports reporter in the early 1960s.
He remembers asking the Great DiMaggio for a favor:

A few days earlier, I'd seen Joe DiMaggio lunching at an
Italian restaurant on Park Avenue. I'd said hello to him
and he'd said hello to me . . . I found out the hotel where
he was staying and took a very long shot. The hotel operator put my call straight through to his room. My heart
was doing somersaults as I waited for him to answer.

"Joe?" I began when he picked up the phone. "This
is Frank Gifford and I have a request for you and I'll
understand perfectly if you can't do it, but I'm retired
from football now and I'm starting a radio show and I'd
like to have you as my first interview, but like I said
I'd understand if you're too busy to . . ."

"I'd love to, Frank."

". . . do it because I realize how . . . Huh? You
would?"

"Absolutely. Do I come over there, or do you want
to come over here?"

"Uh, what would be easier for you?"

"Whatever is easier for you. If you'd like to come
over here, we can do it right now."

Unbelievable! Ten minutes later, I'm standing in
Joe DiMaggio's hotel room with my tape recorder
clasped in my sweaty hands. The first thing that struck
me was that he wasn't nearly as tall as I thought. Not
that he looked little, but to me he'd always seemed like
the tallest man on television. Anyway, he couldn't have
been warmer or more gracious. We talked for so long

that we were able to cut the interview into segments and run it nightly over my first five shows.

Though I can't remember what we talked about, I still think about that afternoon. Joe DiMaggio went from hero to legend to myth, and I caught him in the legend period. But what I'll never forget is how lonely he seemed. He didn't care whether I came to his room or he came to the studio, because apparently he had nothing else to do that day. I've been lonely, too, so I know it when I see it. Joe DiMaggio was one of the loneliest men I've ever met.[6]

*White Sox catcher **Gus Zernial**:*

Joe D. was a very self-centered guy. He didn't talk to anybody. He didn't associate with very many people. He was very much a loner. That had nothing to do with his baseball ability. I hit a lot of long fly balls that he tracked down, and some were hit over his head. He was a tremendous ballplayer. But his personality didn't lend anything to anything. He didn't have a personality.

***Louis Almada**, who played against DiMaggio in the Pacific Coast League in the thirties, played golf with him in the fifties and sixties:*

I would call Charlie Rubalcava. He was a commercial photographer. Joe liked to go to a place, a restaurant, called Beano's. Charlie would call Beano and say, "Lou Almada's coming up. Is Joe in town? Maybe we can get together." Joe wouldn't cotton up to many people. He liked Charlie. He and Charlie played golf quite a bit.

Joe liked playing at the Presidio. We'd be partners. I could outdrive him a hundred yards. Joe just wanted to hit it straight. He just wanted to be straight, so he hit the ball easy. He just wasn't a natural golfer the way he was a natural, great ballplayer.

Willie Mays tried to break into our foursome once. He was out there after the season was over. He said, "Let me join you guys." Joe said no way. We were getting ready to tee off and Willie Mays wanted to join us. Joe looked at Charlie right away and shook his head. Charlie just said, "We don't want a fivesome. Thanks, anyway." Joe didn't like Willie Mays. He was cocky. Arrogant.

Sometimes he'd have a putt and he wanted me to look at it. He'd say, "What do you think, Lou?" I'd look at it and say, "Well, Joe, what do *you* think? It's a little bit downhill. You don't want to hit it too hard." He'd say something and I'd say, "I think you're right." I wouldn't ever tell him how to play it. Because if it went wrong, he wouldn't talk to you for the rest of the game. Charlie told me, "Don't tell him anything. Ask him what he thinks." So I'd just say, "Joe, I think you've got the right idea."

He wasn't a mixer at all. When we got through playing golf, we would sit down to have a bite or have a beer. Joe would just come in and not even say, "See you fellas later. Goodbye." He'd just come in and look at everybody there and just walk away.

⌒

*Writer **Roy Blount Jr.** remembers asking the Great DiMaggio for a small favor in 1968:*

I was doing a story about Danny Cater, then an Oakland A, and DiMaggio at the time was an Oakland vice president and coach. It hurt me to see the Yankee Clipper in that awful looking green and gold uniform and huge white shoes, but I went up to him and asked him about Cater, and he said, "You'd better ask the manager about that."

That's all. I replied, "I've already talked to the manager," and to that DiMaggio had no response at all. In retrospect, it occurs to me that it would have been no more than decent to say something like, "Well, I'm sorry, I don't have anything to say about Danny Cater, but I wish you well in your researches; goodbye, now, I'm busy staring out over the diamond."

He didn't say that, though. He didn't say anything. This was Joe DiMaggio, and I figured he had his reasons.[7]

⌒

John McNamara, *a rookie coach with the Oakland Athletics in 1968:*

He took a liking to me the first day I went into spring training in Bradenton, Florida. I went to my locker, and who am I dressing next to but Mr. DiMaggio. There was a furnace or wall heater between me and the next locker so I just moved over and gave him all the room he wanted.

He was very quiet. Could be very moody. He was always nice and kind to me. He was a very private person. Whatever things were on his mind, he never discussed.

He helped me out. When we played the Twins in Orlando, Billy Martin was their third-base coach. So he called Billy and we went up to Orlando early. He had Billy Martin come over and we sat in the third-base bleachers and had Billy Martin explain to me the duties of coaching third base.

～

Former Saint Louis Browns first baseman **Chuck Stevens**, *who remained active in baseball as head of the Association of Professional Ballplayers of America, remembers Joe DiMaggio—silver haired and decades into retirement—mixing with the public at various baseball functions:*

Most people were so in awe of him, they were uncomfortable. That's the way it is when you meet the president of the United States. It's startling. It's hard to describe.

You gotta realize, this guy labored under the heaviest of burdens. When he was out in public, he had no time when he wasn't under the magnifying glass. For instance, when baseball's winter meetings were held in

Mexico City, I bumped into him in the lobby. We shook hands and hugged, and he said, "Let's go get a cup of tea." So he and I walk to the coffee shop at the Maria Isabella Hotel and we are in the coffee shop, in the back. The man could not drink his tea because of street kids dashing in, looking at him, asking for autographs. These were all Mexicans, but they knew who he was. It got to be kind of scary. We had to leave.

Anywhere he went, Joe would walk in and he'd be having a cocktail and he'd be interrupted five hundred times. He couldn't hang around. As a result, he'd have to leave the party early. And I know he didn't want to. And because Joe left early, had to leave early for comfort and sanity, he'd get badmouthed for that.

I'll never forget, we were in Buffalo. They had opened a new ballpark. There was a big party with lots of people, and Joe came up and was thoroughly enjoying himself and a lady came over and was gushing over him and spilled her drink all over him. He was very gracious. But he had to leave.

Former teammate and San Diego Padres broadcaster **Jerry Coleman**:

During the All-Star Game in San Diego, he was sitting up next to the broadcast booth, and I was working. I went over and started to chew the fat with him. Pretty soon, one of the hotshots around there spotted Joe, and started bringing his friends in to meet Joe. I'm looking at Joe and he's ticked off and he says, "One more, and I'm outta here." That's the way he was. He didn't like to be pestered.

I remember in Anaheim, they had a day with Joe, and Vince, and Dominic. The brothers got together and Joe had to get to the airport. I gave him a ride. What do you do when you get to the airport—you drop the guy off and keep going, right? He said, "Hey, you gotta come in with me." You see, he hated to be alone because he needed somebody to buffer the situation. If he walked into an airport alone, he knew he'd be pestered.

~

Al Gionfriddo, *who caught the ball at the fence and made Joe DiMaggio kick the dirt, remembers him on the baseball card show circuit in the eighties and nineties:*

He and I became good friends. Everyone knocked DiMaggio about being a loner. I hated to see people write things bad about him. Just because a man is a loner, that doesn't say he's a bad person. He liked to lead his life the way he liked to lead his life the same as you like to lead your life. Joe had his own life.

I remember one show, this guy brought a cardboard cutout of him, life-size, full-size. He said, "Joe, I'll pay you for this, will you please sign it?" Joe said, "No. I'm only signing what the manager of the show wanted me to sign, and what the promoter wanted me to sign." You did what the promoter wanted you to do. The promoter's paying you twenty-five thousand for Saturday, and twenty-five thousand for Sunday. So he went along with that.

Every time I wanted him to sign an autograph for me, he never refused. People say he didn't want to sign autographs, he wanted to be paid for it. You can't blame him for that. He made more signing autographs than when he played for the Yankees.

Jeffrey Lyons, son of New York Post columnist Leonard Lyons, remembers his father's old friend:

I was at a baseball card show when my son was nine. DiMaggio was signing. We sent word up that we were there and we wanted to say hello. He stopped the people on line and I walked over with my son, Ben, and he pushed me away gently, and just put his arm around Ben, out of my hearing.

They spoke for fifteen minutes. I said, "What did he do?"

My son said, "He told me what you were like, Dad, at my age."

Diane Cameron was in Towson, Maryland, in 1982, helping her husband run a baseball card show at the

Holiday Inn. She remembers her marriage was crumbling, and she was distracted when she met Joe DiMaggio:

Joe was the guest signer. I was twenty-nine. My job was helping. I had done a number of these shows. My job was to sit with Joe. He had a sort of driver-helper looking out for him. I was also another buffer.

I remember the rules of the road. People paid something like ten dollars for two autographs. And it couldn't be anything with Marilyn on it. That was the ground rule. I didn't understand that then. But I've since understood what that sensitivity was.

I knew he was a famous guy. I knew he was a big, big deal. But not being a serious baseball fan, I didn't quite get what other people in the room were getting about him. Except that he was this incredibly gracious, kind man. One of my memories is sitting beside him and watching him talk to kids. Also realizing that little kids especially didn't know who he was. They knew he was a famous baseball card more than he was a baseball memory. And he would look at them and was just so patient and kind. I thought about this later: How many times in his life did somebody say to him, "Oh, remember this? Remember that?" I imagine it would be so boring after a while. And he never let on that he had answered that question nine million times.

I can remember feeling this without seeing it. I was sitting beside him, and he would be very warm and chatting, and he'd say, "And who are you?" to little kids, and then he would stiffen. I remember looking down and his hand was on top of a picture and he slid it toward me for the person to take on the way out. It was pictures of Marilyn. He didn't say a thing.

He was supposed to be interviewed by a reporter, who was late. There was a room set aside for that. And he said to me, "Come and have your lunch with me." He clearly wasn't so reclusive that he wanted to sit alone in a hotel room and eat. He wanted some company. I think part of being good enough company is that he knew I wasn't going to pester him.

I remember being kind of scared. How was I going to talk to this guy for an hour? And I was in such a bad state, because my marriage was coming apart, that morning I had gotten a diagnosis that scared me about my health—I was just sort of possessed with myself. I was in a bad mood.

What shifted was, he took charge of the situation. I didn't have to entertain him. He talked to me. He asked me all about myself. I don't think I cried, but I do remember going on and on about myself. And he was very kind about that.

All of a sudden it was like sitting down with an uncle or somebody. He sort of implied that he had had hard times, too. What a kind person he was, with a complete stranger. He clearly had this generous capacity with people. I was pouring out all this stuff. I remember him being very comforting.

When Joltin' Joe did it his way at the plate, the swing was level and the result more often than not was a line drive. (AP/Wide World Photos)

His Way

Sam Suplizio, who was mentored by DiMaggio as a
Yankee prospect in the 1950s, remembers the dark side of
his hero:

He was a very angry man. A bitter man. I could see that,
but I'd never say it. He was too much of an idol to me.

I went up to get an autograph on a ball. In a clubhouse. It was about 1984. I was coaching with the
Brewers. I went in there after one of the Old Timers
games with a pen in hand and a ball. I walked back into
the coaches' room.

Man, he wouldn't do it. He said, "No, I'm not signing. I won't sign." He shrugged me away. There I am,
I'm in uniform with the visiting team. Discourteous.
At the time, I figured he was just pressured. I gave him
the benefit of the doubt. Because I had great respect
for him. You don't lose that great respect for a man of
his stature.

⌒

Boston Herald reporter Stephen Harris was covering the
1989 World Series between the Oakland Athletics and the
San Francisco Giants when an earthquake struck, killing
sixty-two.

DiMaggio was in town, and Harris remembers search-
ing the city for him:

The morning after the earthquake, I called the office
to see what they wanted me to do. (Executive sports

editor) Bob Sales had just got a call from Dominic DiMaggio, saying "I'm very worried about my brother Joe and my sister. They have a townhouse right in the Marina District, where there was so much damage, and we can't get hold of them."

So that was my job, to go find Joe DiMaggio. The problem was, I couldn't even get into the area. The area was cordoned off for many blocks. I had to go to three different entry points before I was able to talk my way in. I basically explained to some cop what I was doing, and I think he took pity on me for having to try to find Joe DiMaggio in the middle of all that chaos.

I was talking to a lot of people in his neighborhood. They all kind of said the same thing: "Yeah, we know Joe. He's always around. He's a friendly guy. He's quiet. But he's friendly. Everyone knows him. We all like him very much."

I got to the closest point to where his house was. His house was located on a street that was right at the point where some of the worst damage happened. There was a house right across the street that sort of pancaked down on top of itself, totally destroyed. Right on his corner, about three doors down, an eight-unit apartment building exploded because of a gas main. Several people got killed, I think.

I got within a half a block of his house and I started saying to people, "Have you seen Joe DiMaggio?" Some of them were very friendly, and some of them were like, "You reporters—why don't you leave the poor guy alone?" But one guy said to me, "Yeah, Joe's right over there. I just saw him." And he turned around and pointed to a corner and he wasn't there. He said, "Oh, geez, he was just there a second ago. I don't know where he went."

So I waited. Within a couple of minutes, here he comes, walking down the street. He looked like Joe DiMaggio. So I walked up to him. I introduced myself. He was obviously very preoccupied and distracted. He said to me, "I'm sorry, but I'm looking for my sister. We haven't been able to find her yet. She's very old and we're worried about her."

He was about to walk away from me, and I said, "Joe, I think you were friends with my parents back in the old days in New York." He stopped. I told him, "Curly Harris and Pat Harris." He stopped and looked at me and a smile kind of came on his face, and he said, "Yeah. You know, I can see the resemblance." He said "How are they doing?" and I said they were okay.

And he said, "Okay, what do you want to know?"

~

Jack Lang, veteran newspaperman and top man of the Baseball Writers Association of America, remembers DiMaggio, in his late seventies and still on guard:

He was appearing at the New York Baseball Writers dinner to receive an award that we had inaugurated in his name, the Joe DiMaggio Toast of the Town Award. Each year we honor somebody as the biggest name in New York sports. We started it in about 1990.

I Remember Joe DiMaggio

He called me up on the Sunday afternoon. He was in the same hotel. He was upstairs on the fiftieth floor, and I was on the forty-fourth or something. He called me up and said, "What am I supposed to say?" He said, "Why don't you write a little something for me to say and I'll say it?" I said, "Sure." So I typed out a little acceptance speech on an index card and I sent it up to his room. About ten minutes later, he called up and said, "That's good. But I'd like to change a few things. Can I come down to your suite and we'll go over it?" I said yeah. He said, "Is there anybody there?" I said, "No, I'm all alone."

In between the time I told him that and he came down, my two teenage sons arrived to attend the dinner that night. Joe walks in the room and he stopped and he said, "I thought you told me nobody was here." I said, "Joe, these are my sons. They just arrived." Well, he agreed to stay for a few minutes and we went over the speech. But the mere fact that somebody was in the room was enough that he was going to walk back out again. He didn't want anybody around him unless he needed somebody. He wanted his privacy.

Boston Herald *columnist* **George Kimball** *remembers dining with* New York Daily News *boxing writer Michael Katz at a pub in Atlantic City, New Jersey, before covering a bout at the Convention Center. They were summoned upstairs to sit down with the eighty-two-year-old Joe DiMaggio:*

You would have had to see this pub and this house. The whole place was right out of the 1930s. The furniture and the whole place. And they had this inn upstairs, where they rent rooms. Like a thirties boarding house. The whole place was like your grandmother's attic.

The owner's wife just comes down and says, "Come on upstairs. I've got a surprise for you." These old guys sitting around in their undershirts, having coffee and breadsticks. Joe was in his shirtsleeves.

He wanted to talk about the Oscar De La Hoya–Pernell Whitaker fight earlier that year. And he wanted to talk about the fight that night. He was surprisingly knowledgeable about boxing. I was surprised at how much he knew. His questions were very thoughtful.

⁓

Dino Restelli, *who grew up to play for the Pirates*:

I was born and raised in Saint Louis, Missouri. I saw all the big-league teams come through Sportsman's Park. I was a fan of his. And when we moved to San Francisco, even more so.

I was living on Telegraph Hill in San Francisco. The year he had his fifty-six-game hitting streak, we used to come home from school with a buddy of mine who lived right next door to us, and the first thing we used to do was go to the village grocery store and look at the paper to see if he had gotten another base hit.

I went to Galileo High School. That's where Joe had started. His brother Dominic went there. The whole baseball team, every day, we used to come in and get the morning paper or go to the library. The whole baseball team was into this record. We followed it very closely. When it ended, we were very disappointed. It felt like it was going to go on forever.

It's not that I copied my stance like his, but I did have a similar stance. As a matter of fact, Charlie Graham, the owner of the San Francisco Seals, made a statement when they signed me to a contract. He said, "I think we signed another Joe DiMaggio." Oh, gosh. I was walking on air.

There weren't many big-league Italians that stood out and were stars. As a matter of fact, we used to put Italian names on the players, like Babe Ruth and Gehrig—you know, we'd call them Ruthelli. Because we wanted Italian heroes.

We moved to San Francisco when I was about thirteen. We moved to North Beach, where Joe was brought up. He was born in Martinez, but he grew up in North Beach. The house that we lived in was about four doors from the DiMaggios.

As a kid coming and going from school I used to see the DiMaggio brothers during the off-season. I got to see them quite often. I talked to them. I mean, when you're a kid, you've got more guts than a rattlesnake.

The first time I talked to Joe was at the North Beach playground. He came down there during the off-season and he was just sort of hanging around with his buddies. We were playing softball. Everybody played at the North Beach playground. I just went over and said, "Hello, Mr. DiMaggio." I was too young to be that brazen. He said, "Hi, how are you, what's your name?" And I told him.

And he never forgot it. All the years later that I would see him, no matter where I would see him, he would always address me, "Dino. It's nice to see you."

When I was a kid, they used to put on a day at the races for him, because he was a real race buff. At Golden Gate Field. He would sit there and we would ask him for autographs and he would sign autographs. You know, it never ceases to amaze me. People say he wouldn't sign an autograph unless you paid him 150 bucks or whatever it was. I'll bet I got ten or twelve autographs from Joe. He signed everything for me.

⁓

*Retired aerospace executive **Bernie Esser** recalls his friendship with the aging DiMaggio:*

In 1941, I was ten years old. I was San Franciscan. He was my hero and I would climb on a streetcar, on the back where you could sneak on, and go downtown to find out whether he had continued his streak. I go to the newspaper stands. I go take a look and go home and nobody was the wiser. I knew before anybody whether he did or he didn't get his hit.

I'm a book collector. I have close to four thousand books on baseball. In 1982, I had a book about

Cooperstown by Marty Appel. It was set up with two columns of print and a middle column with a picture and a big white space that said, "You ought to put an autograph here" to me. That started an adventure that really is unbelievable.

I wrote Joe this letter. In '82, I was fifty-two. I had not gotten a baseball autograph since I was a kid. It all started this way. Highpockets George Kelly, the Giants first baseman who's in the Hall of Fame, was a neighbor of mine. I took this silly book over to him and he signed it. Lefty Gomez. I stopped by his house and he signed. Berra came out with the Yankees and I got him to sign it. I went back to Kelly and said, "Look at this, I got three Hall of Famers."

Then I got four. I got DiMaggio.

The way I got him, I wrote him a letter. He was very nice to me. He said, "Give me a call," and he gave me the number at the restaurant. And we arranged a meeting. And we met. And that started a friendship that was very modest until he started banking at the bank that I bank in. From that point on, we became pretty good friends. I went to his house, he came to my house. We went out to lunches and dinners. Not to any great extent, but when it was acceptable to him and myself.

In different environments, he acted different ways. For example, I'd come into the bank and he'd be sitting there with the bank manager. And he'd call me over and we'd sit and chew the fat. He was always being given opportunities, two thousand bats and this sort of stuff. He'd have a proposal, and he'd ask me what I thought of it. That just really boggled my mind, that he would consider my opinion worthwhile.

He was very attuned to politics. He had his likes and he had his dislikes. There were times, when we would go down to San Jose, where there was a restaurant that he really, really liked. It's about a fifty-mile drive. I'd go to his place and pick him up and we might talk a little bit, we might not. He was enraptured with his granddaughters. He just thought the world of them. We'd talk about them.

I never, ever brought up Marilyn Monroe. I had no need to know. He had a portrait of her over his sofa in the front room. In his house. It was a beautiful portrait. I did say once, "They really did a good job on that one." He said, "Yes. They did." And that was all there was to it.

He was quiet, but he wasn't afraid to express his opinion. He had a lot of interests. He was a big buff on movies and on stage plays. In fact, the first time I met him, when I was up in his restaurant, I was going to New York for the first time in my life, with my wife for our twenty-fifth wedding anniversary. Joe talked about how Walter Winchell was very influential in his day, and how Joe would go with him because Winchell could get better seats than Joe could get. He liked music. The music of the forties.

He really liked my wife. He never addressed her by her first name. Always "Mrs. Esser." I never once paid for a meal that I had with Joe. I wished today that I had asked for the little slip that he got from his credit card to prove that, hey, he didn't have short arms. In my experience with the man, that just wasn't a characteristic of him. But everybody says he was the opposite.

We have an old-time baseball group that meets once a month. I'm one of the young ones, and I'm seventy. Joe did not come back to his old neighborhood. And why should he? He wasn't overly friendly and they took it as snobbery on his part and it really wasn't.

He was always meticulously dressed—never disheveled. The idea that you had to dress a certain way for him? That's just garbage. Ted Williams, when I was a little guy, was my hero in one respect: He wouldn't wear a tie. I ended up wearing a tie for a long time. But when I went out with Joe, there was no way I would put a tie on. Nor did I even think about it. I would wear a sport coat and a sport shirt and a pair of slacks. He would have a tie on, but I never wore a tie around the man.

I can't think of anything that hasn't been written about him, in terms of goods and bads and pros and cons. I was pretty upset by this latest book. I didn't think that did justice to Joe. When he passed away, I was curious as to how many of his autographs I had. And it's over a hundred, in all kinds of different books. And then there's pictures—there's all kinds of stuff. And I never paid a nickel for any of it. He was most gracious.

Esser, *like many of DiMaggio's cronies, recalls a strange turn toward the end. And like many of DiMaggio's cronies,*

His Way

he blames attorney Morris Engelberg, who ran DiMaggio's business affairs in the last years of DiMaggio's life:

The last time that Joe and I had contact was probably around 1995 or 1996.

I have two grandchildren. And when they were born, I was around Joe and he signed balls to each of them, "Your grandfather is a good friend of mine," and he put the date of birth on there.

Subsequent to that, a few years later, my daughter had another child. I had forgotten about this baseball for the kids. She called me one day and said, Did I think I could get Joe to sign one? I said, "Yeah, sure, no problem. I'll get a ball."

He always came out here on Thanksgiving and Christmas to be with his granddaughters. It was during those period of times when normally we got together. My birthday is December 27, and we went out maybe five or six times on my birthday. So anyway, I gave him a call on this Thanksgiving and the first thing he said was, "How did you know I was in town?" I should have known better than that there was something amiss. But I didn't. I said, "Joe, you always come into town this week." He said, "Well, what do you want?" He was very curt to me. I said, "A couple of years ago, you signed some baseballs for my grandchildren. Now I've got one new one. And I'd like to get a ball signed by you." And he said, "Well, what about books?" I said, "Well, I'm sure I've got some books around here that you haven't autographed." He said, "I find that hard to believe." I said, "Well, they keep writing them, Joe." There was a little levity there. He said, "You don't have that Durso book, do you?" I said, "Yeah, I got that." He said, "I won't sign that."

The Durso book was one where there was a contract with the publisher for a million dollars or something. And Joe agreed to it. And when Durso meant him to begin the book, he began with Marilyn first, and Joe said, "No way, no how."

I said, "I have a few others, Joe, that would be nice, if you wouldn't mind." And he said, "I've got to call my attorney." That just didn't make any sense to me at all. He said, "Call me tomorrow."

So the next morning, I called him. And he said, "I can sign two books for you. The one my brother wrote and the one that Tommy Henrich wrote." I didn't want his autograph in those—I wanted Dom and Tom. He said, "Well, those are the only ones I'll sign." And I said, "I really didn't call you about books. I called you about a baseball." He said, "Yeah, I'll sign the baseball. When will you be here?" I said, "I'll be there in a half-hour." So I jumped in the car and took my ball and off I went.

When I got there, I rang the doorbell. He lived on a street where the houses were attached. He had a gate so the only place you could stay was out on the sidewalk in front of his house unless he pushed the buzzer and you went up. I rang the doorbell and nothing happened and I'm standing out there like a jackass. An old fart standing out on the street at 8:30 in the morning. I felt very uncomfortable.

I thought, *Hey, he stiffed me*, and I started to walk away. He stayed on the third floor of the house and he knocked on the window and waved for me to come back. So I did. A little while later, the front door opens and he calls down, "I'll be down in a few minutes." Any other time I was at his house, he'd open the gate and I would come up to the house.

The next thing I know, the garage door opens and Joe pulls his car out. And he parked over the sidewalk and went in and hit the buzzer and the door closed. I hadn't noticed, but there was a little patch of ground and there was a little plant in there, and lo and behold, there's a baseball in the plant. And he picks this thing up and he says, "They're *always* leaving these god—— things around." He put it out on the sidewalk. He goes over and he climbs into his car. And I thought he was going to leave. And I'm standing there with my stupid baseball. He said, "What have you got for me to sign?" I said, "The ball, Joe." And he signed it. This time I didn't get, "Your grandfather is a good friend of mine." I didn't have the guts to ask him about that. I just wanted to get my ball and get the hell out of there.

He signs the ball, and as he's backing out, he rolls down the window, and he said, "Bernie, I got my problems, too." And he drove away.

This was just so totally out of character. One time, I took a suitcase full of books for him to sign and he did it. He was in my house and I got him to sign tons of books. To have this total change in character. We were good friends. He liked me. I never understood why. He treated me better than most people. Charlie Silvera, the

145

old Yankee catcher, is a neighbor of mine and Charlie will tell you, I knew Joe better than *he* did. For some reason, he took this liking to me. And that day was totally out of character.

I didn't know what to think. He had called me about a year before this. I was a vice president of an aerospace company. I was having a big meeting and I told my secretary, "No calls." And DiMaggio called. So she opened the door and told me that he's on the phone. I was really upset because I had people in there, and I didn't have the time to be talking to Joe. And so he wanted to go to lunch and I couldn't. I was a little curt. I had heard, "All it takes is one," and down the drain you go with Joe. So when he treated me this way, the only thing I could think of was that lunch that I didn't go to.

But after he passed away, I saw Bill Madden, the writer from the *Daily News*, a very good friend of mine. Barry Halper and Joe had their tiff. Talking with Madden and Halper, it became obvious to me that the problem wasn't me, the problem was Joe's lawyer, Morris Engelberg. You know, "I got to call my lawyer." That just didn't make any sense to me.

When Joe went in the hospital, one day they're giving him the last rites, the next day they're saying he's going to go play golf in the morning. It was really stupid. Engelberg just really pissed me off. I wrote him a letter and told him, "If you're truly a friend of DiMaggio, don't seek publicity, you keep your mouth shut. I have a suggestion for you. Keep your big mouth shut." And I signed it. Two days later I got a two-page, typewritten thing in ExpressMail that told me I didn't know what I was talking about and he was Joe's savior, he had spent the last seventy days with Joe and it cost his firm two hundred thousand dollars. That kind of clued me in that it wasn't me.

Engelberg had convinced Joe that anyone who wanted something from him was trying to use him. And I wasn't. These books, anything I have signed by him, my kids are going to have. You couldn't buy one from me. There isn't a price on it.

In terms of the last time I was around him, it wasn't so pleasant. But I had such a wonderful ten years or so with the man. I miss him. I missed him even before he passed away.

I was a nobody and he treated me like a somebody. I wish I had one more chance to talk to him like we used to talk.

Joe Vetrano Jr. recalls Joe DiMaggio's relationship with his father, former San Francisco 49er Joe "the Toe" Vetrano:

My dad and Joe met each other back in the fifties. My dad was a football player. He was with the original 49ers and he coached with the Niners in the fifties. And then he coached college football at Southern Mississippi in the sixties. They were big golfing pals. They used to play quite a bit with Lefty O'Doul. Lefty was a very good friend of my dad and of Joe.

This is the silver-haired Joe DiMaggio that most baby boomers, too young to have seen him play but familiar with his Mr. Coffee persona, remember. (AP/Wide World Photos)

My first recollection of him is when I was about five years old, something like that. In the mid-sixties. As a little kid, I used to go with them. At least once a week, I'd go out and play golf with them, or at least drive the golf cart. They would just go play golf and go to the racetrack together and do all the normal things guys do.

My dad loved to laugh. It seemed like they were always laughing, having a good time. Joe had great knowledge of the horse races, but Joe wasn't a big gambler. Joe would wait until he had a for-sure thing and bet a few bucks on it. He would win more times than not. But he didn't like to go out and make a big bet. He enjoyed it. He enjoyed athletics. He enjoyed competition. He loved to play golf. He liked to get out there and get involved in different games with people.

He loved to play golf. They'd play a lot of scrambles. When he was in town, which back then was all the time, they'd play at least once or twice a week at Half Moon Bay. They'd go down there and get into some money matches. And have a lot of fun.

He was a very loyal guy. He would never say anything bad about anybody. For him to say something bad about somebody was very unusual. He would just kind of observe and hold it in. He and my dad would talk privately about things. They would never talk about important private issues around me. I'd hear them start to talk about things, and essentially my dad would dismiss me. They had a lot of private conversations. Joe was a very private guy who didn't let down his guard often.

His big thing was always, "anticipate." I think if there's one thing that made him so great as a ballplayer, he used to always tell me as a child, whether it was in playing Little League baseball or in business, that you always need to anticipate what's going to happen next. That's what he did in the outfield. He always anticipated. He wasn't the fastest guy, but he anticipated where the ball was going to be hit. That's why I believe he got such great jumps on everything.

He'd talk to me. Joe wasn't a guy who'd sit you down and give you lectures. But I spent enough time with him where we'd have conversations. They were always from the heart. Just life experiences. We'd talk golf, we'd talk baseball. Growing older, his big thing was he enjoyed kids. He didn't mind about giving to children. He liked to help children.

He used to come to my baseball games. He and my dad would sit up in the car and watch from the left-field fence. If Joe was in town, he'd always go to the games. He gave me my first baseball glove. He gave me a Joe DiMaggio baseball glove. And then when I'd get done with the games, he would critique me. No matter what I did, he would say, "You did that really well. But were you thinking of this . . ." He liked to teach. I just always remember Joe trying to make me a better baseball player, but at the same time he wasn't overbearing with it. He just gave me the information. If you took it, you took it.

You see these people now who are badmouthing him. "Oh, he wouldn't give me an autograph." Joe would sign a ball for any kid, at any time, at any place. I saw this. I saw him where he would get mad, or when he wouldn't want to do it—it would be when he saw these adults come up with four pictures and they'd want an autograph, and they were going to turn around and sell them. I'd see it time and time again. People would come up and say, "Could you sign this?" And Joe would say, "Well, who would you like me to sign it to?" They'd say, "Oh, I don't want a name on it." That would drive him crazy. As he grew older, I think it was pretty plain and simple—he just got tired of being used.

Like all famous athletes that you were around, and he was one of the biggest, he never had a moment to himself, where he didn't have somebody demanding something. That's one of the things that's so tiresome now. You have all these people calling him different names, or saying that he wasn't generous with his time. If it was for a child, he would do it. For the adults, it wasn't always the case.

They had a rift. I don't remember how many years. It was just a misunderstanding. It was something golf-related. It was over something that wasn't that serious. And them both being stubborn Italians, neither one of them would admit that they were wrong. My dad wouldn't apologize to Joe and Joe wouldn't apologize to my dad. And one day Joe called my dad up and asked him if he wanted to go to the horse races. And they started palling around again together.

My dad was always pretty healthy. Then he had a heart condition and he had a stroke. I can't remember if Joe was in New York or Florida. But Joe was back east when I called him and told him. He flew out immediately. He spent quite a bit of the time in the hospital with him.

When my dad was sick, Joe was in the hospital with me. It was just another perfect example of what he goes through. We're standing in front of the door where my dad was dying, in intensive care, and we're teary eyed. And you've got people coming by, gawking at him and saying, "Are you Joe DiMaggio?" He just didn't have privacy. He knew who he was and what he had to deal with. It wasn't an easy thing.

My dad came home from the hospital. And Joe would come over to visit. I can remember how many days my dad was home—maybe four or five. It wasn't more than a week. Joe would come over to the house and they would sit in front of the house and just talk about whatever they liked to talk about. They would just sit and reflect and talk. One day they drove down to see a good friend of theirs who was the pro at Half Moon Bay. My dad knew he was going to pass away. He wanted to go down there one last time. They went down there and putted.

When they got back that day, they were sitting in front of my parents' house in San Francisco. They were on two foldout chairs in the driveway. They were just sitting there. My dad just leaned over to Joe and said, "Joe, I'm going." And Joe said, "Where we going?" Because my dad was always joking. And my dad said, "No, I'm going." And my dad just fell into Joe's arms. He died in his arms.

That's why it's so upsetting to hear all these negative things. It was hard for Joe to be in public, just being Joe DiMaggio. But when that happened, Joe did everything he could for our family. He asked if he could help with the funeral arrangements. He went with us in the limo. He wanted to help my mom. He called my mom just about every day for a week, just to make sure she was okay. He was very compassionate.

DiMaggio was already a legend in his own time from his baseball exploits alone, but his marriage to screen star Marilyn Monroe assured Joe's celebrity status for posterity. (AP/Wide World Photos)

HARPO SPEAKS

"My husband would get into moods where he wouldn't talk to me for seven or eight days. One time it was ten days."[1]

—MARILYN MONROE on Joe DiMaggio

He didn't talk a lot to Marilyn, or his teammates, or the press, but Joe DiMaggio went on the record more often than your average recluse. He was no J. D. Salinger or Howard Hughes. He merely preferred to speak on his own terms, on the subjects that he preferred to talk about. A collection of DiMaggio utterances:

⌒

On his earliest memories of baseball:

It's funny how your perspective changes. When I was a little fellow in San Francisco, I used to look at the wire screen atop the right-field wall in old Recreation Park and think what a tremendous distance it was from the plate. But when I got older and played an exhibition game there, it didn't seem so far away anymore.

It thrilled me as a kid to see guys like Smead Jolley, Ike Boone, Lefty O'Doul, and Ping Bodie— Ping was on his way down then—bounce them off the chicken wire.

I once made a catch in that ballpark, one I never can forget. I was about twelve years old, and I was in the bleachers when Hollis Thurston belted a homer. I leaped out of my seat and caught the ball after it cleared the fence.

As you know, I broke into pro ball as a shortstop for the San Francisco Seals in the last week of the 1933 season. I could catch the ball but I never could find the first baseman with my throws. The next year I went in as a pinch-hitter, walked on four straight pitches, and made ready to go to the clubhouse at the end of the inning. My brother, Vince, stopped me and nodded toward Ike Caveney, our manager.

"Ike wants you to go to the outfield," he said.

I never left it.[2]

On his most embarrassing moment on the baseball field:

The time I got hit on the head by a fly ball, playing a night game with the San Francisco Seals. There were a lot of bugs in the lights that night. I chased a bug instead of a ball.

By the time I spotted the bug that wasn't buzzing, it was too late—the fly ball bounced off the side of my head. The fans didn't heckle me. It was my hometown.

But I remember a fellow named Jode Fenton, the first baseman on the other team, did heckle me. He just pointed at me and roared.

Next night, I got my innings. It was a windy night, and when one of the Seals knocked up a pop fly, Fenton yelled, "I got it. I got it. All mine." He stood right under it. Then the wind took it away. He followed across the pitcher's mound, still yelling, "All mine." But the wind kept dragging it away as it came down. Fenton made a dive to snag it across third base, but sure enough, *clunk*, it caught him right on the head.

Everybody was grinning, but I was roaring, "Yeah, you got it all right, you sure did." Fenton turned beet red in the face and stomped off the field. Couldn't stand it. And I knew just how he felt.[3]

On his voyage from San Francisco to Saint Petersburg, Florida, to report to his first spring training with the Yankees:

Frankie Crosetti and Tony Lazzeri, fellow San Franciscans and already established Yankee stars, agreed to chaperone me across the country. After all, I had never been east of the Rockies, and they weren't so certain that I was bright enough to buy a ticket, get on a train, and reach Saint Pete all in one piece. I was grateful for their solicitude because it saved me from entering the Yankee camp cold. Their presence would give me some moral support when I reported to Joe McCarthy.

I was really seeing America for the first time on that trip. Any ballplayer is likely to remember always his first trip to a big-league training camp, but this one stood out in my mind because of its accent on silence. I had already been called Dead Pan by a couple of sportswriters, and neither Crosetti nor Lazzeri was exactly a barber. We went two or three hundred miles at a clip without any of us saying a word.

Near the end of the first day, Tony asked me to relieve Frankie at the wheel.

"I'm sorry," I said as meekly as I could, "but I don't drive."

"You don't what?" screamed Lazzeri.

"Let's throw the bum out," said Crosetti.

They didn't, of course, but they gave me a couple of twelve-pound looks from time to time during the remainder of the trip.[4]

~

On his arrival at his first Yankee spring training camp:

I was nearly frightened to death. I took a look at those big fellows, big in size as well as in name. There were guys like Bill Dickey, Lou Gehrig, Red Ruffing, and Lefty Gomez. I just froze.[5]

Tony (Lazzeri) brought me in the Yankee clubhouse and introduced me around. Those famous Yankees awed me. Lou Gehrig gave me a warm welcome, but Red Ruffing—I didn't learn until later that he was a great needler—gave me the business.

"If you can hit .398 on the coast," he said, "you should hit at least .450 in this league. We have better lights and we play with new white balls that are easy to see." What a great group they were, especially after I got to know them.[6]

~

On what life was like for him while being married to Marilyn Monroe:

My life is dull. I never interfere with Marilyn's work. I don't go to the studios to see her act. It's the same stuff all the time. You see only a little of it. Shoot a scene—then hang around for the last ones. I wait and see the pictures.

I get up early and play golf. The best round I ever shot was 83. I'm improving every day.

I bought her a set of clubs. She takes a hell of a cut. She hits a long ball when she hits it.

She was working hard long before she met me. And for what? What has she got after all these years? Don't think it's easy work, acting in the movies. She works like a dog. It's hard work. When she's working she's up at five or six in the morning and doesn't get through until around seven. Then we eat dinner, watch a little television, and go to sleep.

We're people who don't go out much. We don't go to parties. We don't get mixed up in many crowds.[7]

On Vince, Dom, and him playing in the major leagues:

If anyone wants to know why three kids in one family made it to the big leagues, they just had to know how we helped each other and how much we practiced back then. We did it every minute we could.[8]

During his holdout in the spring of 1938, during which he missed the first twelve days of the regular season, a reporter found DiMaggio at his family's restaurant on Fisherman's Wharf in San Francisco. A word-by-word account of the ensuing interview:

Reporter: Have you contacted Ruppert?
DiMaggio: Nope.
Reporter: Will you accept twenty-five thousand dollars?
DiMaggio: Nope.
Reporter: Will you appeal to Judge Landis?
DiMaggio: Nope.

Reporter: Will you play for anybody?
DiMaggio: Nope.
Reporter: Has Ruppert contacted you recently?
DiMaggio: Nope.
Reporter: Is any settlement looming?
DiMaggio: Nope.
Reporter: Are you doing anything about the situation?
DiMaggio: Nope.[9]

On fan reaction to his 1938 holdout:

It got so I couldn't sleep at night. I'd wake up with the boos ringing in my ears. I'd get up, light a cigarette and walk the floor sometimes till dawn.[10]

On the baseball mitts of his era:

I don't know how I caught anything with the glove I used in 1936. It was just a postage stamp compared to these big things you see now. As a matter of fact, the glove I used in 1951 is completely outmoded. It's amazing what they've done to make it easier to catch baseballs.[11]

I Remember Joe DiMaggio

On his bats:

It's hard not to swing from the heels, but whenever I found myself doing that too much, I'd reach for a heavier bat. The heavy bat and the wide stance I used helped me cut down on my swing.[12]

On his philosophy of hitting:

I look for his fastball. Then if he comes in with a curve, I still have time to swing.[13]

On seeing a glimpse of his roots on a trip to Sicily, when he visited his father's birthplace, the village of Isola Delle Femmine:

I even found two returned immigrants from Martinez, California, who remembered me as a kid there. It's extraordinary how much the two fishing towns resemble each other. I could understand immediately why the DiMaggios were at home in California.[14]

162

On pressure during his famous fifty-six-game hitting streak in 1941:

There was pressure, but I could sleep—when I had the chance. The fans kept knocking on my door.

I was always surrounded by fans, well wishers. Pressure on the field? On the ball field, I felt safest.[15]

On Philadelphia A's pitcher Johnny Babich, who vowed to stop DiMaggio's streak at forty, even if he had to walk him every time up:

He was out to get me, even if it meant walking me every time up. I glanced over on the 3-0 count and McCarthy had given the hit sign. The next pitch was outside, too. But I caught it good and lined it right past Babich into center field for a hit.[16]

Upon breaking Wee Willie Keeler's record by hitting in forty-five straight games:

Well, fellas, when I started this streak, I had no idea it was going to last anywhere near as long as this. When I got up around thirty straight games, I was almost indifferent about it, figuring that if I gave it too much thought I might start pressing and not be natural at the plate. I even told one reporter I hoped I would go oh-for-four if I was going to cause all that commotion. But when I got up to thirty-five games I really got interested in it myself. I said to myself, just like the human fly when he got up to the thirty-fifth floor of the Empire State Building, why not go farther? And that's when I started bearing down.[17]

On the end of his streak:

Well, to get to the final day in Cleveland, I remember this quite well, it was a night ball game and it had rained the day before, which made the field very soggy. I came to the plate the first time against Al Smith, and he walked me on four straight pitches. The second time I came to bat, why, I hit a ball down the third-base line on which Kenny Keltner made a great fielding stop. He knew I wasn't going to bunt, so he played deep in left field, and, actually, when he fielded the ball he was in foul territory and he straightened out and made that long throw to first base and it just nipped me. It was one of those nip-and-tuck plays where the umpire called me out. However, it was very heavy going to first base due to the rain and that's one of the reasons I wasn't able to beat the play.

Of course, the next time I came to bat, I pretty much hit the same kind of a ball where he caught it on kind of a half-hop, brought it into foul territory, and straightened up and threw me out again.

My last time at bat we managed to get Al Smith out of there and Jim Bagby came in to relieve. This time the bags were loaded and I hit a ground ball to Lou Boudreau, the shortstop, and as it was approaching him, the ball took a bad hop, bounded up, and he caught it along his chest. He whipped it over to second—and that was it.

The following day I started another streak. I went on sixteen more games, and I want to tell you something, I could have never stood that pressure again.

Strangely enough, I wanted to keep on going. I felt a little downhearted. I was stopped, but I quickly got over that. It was like going into the seventh game of the World Series, and losing it. That's how I felt. But I did want to keep it going. I wanted it to go on forever.[18]

On his holdout in the spring of 1942, when the Yankees rewarded him for his remarkable 1941 season by offering him a contract with no raise:

I don't like having to wrangle for my salary, but the only contract the club has offered me was for thirty-seven thousand dollars, exactly the same as I got last year.

All I have told (Yankee president Ed) Barrow is that I think I deserve a raise. I didn't give him any figure, so it isn't true that I am holding out for anything exorbitant. I simply said to look at the record and see if I didn't deserve a raise.

165

Did I get a bonus for my batting streak? Ha! I did not. I didn't even get a pat on the back. Nobody even said thank you.

The club made money last year. Barrow admits that. And it won the championship. Now it would be one thing if they offered whatever raise they thought I earned, but I don't think it's fair to send me a contract for the same dough they were offering me a year ago.

Yeah, I know they say it's the usual procedure. But I don't like the usual procedure. I don't want to have to argue for weeks every year for what the club ought to offer in the first place. What's the use in sending me the same contract if they don't even expect me to sign it?

I only want what is fair. I know some of the other players were given raises. I know the club made money and that I helped it. So all I want is to be paid what I'm worth.[19]

On fan reaction to his holdout in the summer of 1942:

Eventually, I signed for $43,750, but while I was battling for it, the Yankee front office put out a lot of propaganda about boys being in the army at twenty-one dollars a month, the insinuation being that I was lucky to be playing ball. I don't think anything burned me up as much as that.

What letters I got after (Yankees chief Ed) Barrow mentioned the soldiers! Baseball owners ruled with an iron hand then. Now, with the free-agent situation, the shoe is on the other foot. And deservedly so.

There were times when it was plain hell. I'd read in the papers the next day that the cheers offset the boos, but you could never prove it by me. All I ever heard were the boos.

At first I thought it would wear off, but it didn't, and every town I went into I'd get a fresh batch of raspberries right between the eyes. And it didn't seem to make any difference whether I had a bad day or a good day. Pretty soon I got the idea that the only reason people came to the game at all was to give DiMaggio the works.

I remember I was going to Saint Louis and we played a Monday game there, and there were only a few scattered hundred in the stands. It was practically an empty house. That was one day I wasn't bothered much. There weren't enough people in the stands to get up a real good boo. It was the first time I ever enjoyed playing in what practically amounted to privacy.[20]

On the causes of batting slumps:

Oh, pressing too hard, hot weather—almost anything. I don't like to talk about slumps.[21]

They were light years apart in personality and style, but Joe DiMaggio and Casey Stengel each achieved a level of cult status and they shared a New York Yankee heritage. Here they are circa 1950. (AP/Wide World Photos)

To newspapermen when he was battling a heel ailment in the spring of 1949:

Don't you think you've gone far enough? You guys are driving me batty. Can't you leave me alone? This affects me mentally too, you know.[22]

⌒

On the heroic June 1949 return to blitz the Red Sox at Fenway Park:

How could I forget it? I'd missed the first sixty-seven games of the season with a bone spur on my heel, and the Yankees hadn't done too well. I was afraid the Red Sox would run away with it, so I decided to come back in that first game in Boston. Fortunately, we won the game and swept the series and got back in the pennant race.[23]

⌒

On the final days of the 1949 season, when the Yankees and Red Sox wrestled for the American League pennant:

Looking back on the old days, I can remember only two times that I ever cried. Once was the day Lou Gehrig said farewell to the club. The second time was late in the season of 1949, the one that began with sixty days of heel grief.

It was ending now with two weeks of the worst flu
virus on record. I had a temperature of 104 degrees,
three nurses, and two doctors. In the midst of my mis-
ery, we got news that Yankee fans were planning the
biggest shindig in my behalf in the team's history: a
bang-up Joe DiMaggio day.

On the day before the ceremony, I was still in bed
with a fever, and the doctors advised me not to go. But
more important than what was being planned for me by
the fans was the fact that we were a game out of first
place with only two remaining games to be played—
against our old rivals, the Red Sox.

Yankee doctors were torn between their affection
for the team and their medical duty. They couldn't
make themselves tell me to get out of bed. But they
wouldn't tell me to miss the game, either. I took the
decision out of their hands.

"If the Yanks are going down," I said, "I'll go down
with them."

I had lost eighteen pounds, and I didn't know if I
could stand up on my own two legs. But the thing that
really had me scared stiff was the fact that I was expect-
ed to make a speech . . .

Anyway, when I walked out onto the field on my
"day"—my uniform shirt already sweated through from
weakness—the fans presented me with a Cadillac, a
speedboat, TV set, radio, gold watches, rings and jewel-
ry. There was a bicycle and a train for little Joe and an
automobile and flowers for Mom. I knew this would be
Mom's last trip anyplace. She had cancer and didn't

know it. This was the day she made that famous crack when somebody interviewed her:

"Which team are you pulling for, Mrs. DiMaggio?"

"I'm pulling for both of them," she said. "Only I want Dom to win because Joe wins so much."

My speech wasn't bad. I excused myself for turning my back on my best friends, the bleacherites, and then I said, "Thank the Good Lord for making me a Yankee."[24]

On playing first base for one game in 1950:

Casey Stengel asked me about it in Boston. "Yeah," I said. "I'll give it a try." I had a week of practice and then the big day came.

I was in a cold sweat every minute. I handled thirteen chances without a boot but I got every play in the book: the 3-6-3 double play, pop flies, cutoffs, and a near triple play. I'd have made it, but Cass Michaels got in line with the throw and it came at me out of his shirt, caroming off my glove. I was never so nervous in my life. Luckily for me, Hank Bauer turned his ankle and I got back to the outfield the next day.[25]

On his career, entering the 1951 season:

I'd like to have a good year and then hang up my spikes. I am not a brittle ballplayer. I never have been. I am a good, tough-boned guy, but I'd rather quit at the top than fade out.[26]

On his slumping hitting skills in the summer of 1951:

I haven't been doing anything to help the club. I just can't seem to buy a base hit. I know what's the matter with me. I'm not getting the old snap in my swing. I just don't seem to give it that old follow through. I just haven't been able to make the bat come around as quick as I used to.

I am swinging late. But it's not because I'm biting at bad balls. I'll go for a bad one now and then. But most of the time, they're right down the middle. I see them coming and I set myself. But when I swing, the ball shoots right up at me.

It's not that I don't know what's the matter with me. I know what I'm doing wrong. It's just that I can't seem to do anything about it. Naturally, I'm concerned, but to a point where it's got me down in the dumps. I'm going to keep swinging until I get the old snap back. It will come back to me. I know it. I'm going to battle it until I lick it.[27]

On his participation in a baseball tour of Japan after the 1951 season:

In November 1951, Lefty O'Doul, manager of the San Francisco Seals, and I made a twenty-five-day postseason junket to baseball crazy Japan and the Korean battlefront. I've always said that Lefty O'Doul could be Emperor of Japan tomorrow if he chose to run. The trip he made with me was his fifth to the Orient.

I went along as the winner of a nationwide poll in which Japanese fans voted for the U.S. player they'd most like to see in action.

They almost didn't see me in action. In fact I was all but killed in a frenzied tickertape, welcoming parade down the Ginza, Tokyo's main drag. There were a million wild-eyed people lining the streets that day, all yelling, screaming, waving banners, and trying to scramble up on our car.

People were hopping on the hood and sliding right up to the windshield aiming cameras at us, and several times I let out a yell, "For God's sake, stop the car! There's somebody under the wheels!"

I was slated to take part in a home run contest against Makoto Kuzuru, Japan's Babe Ruth, the following day and I wanted to get some sleep. Unfortunately, my hotel room happened to be on ground level with the window facing the street. I think all the kids in Tokyo were congregated on the sidewalk, waving little slips of paper, and shouting, "DiMaggio-san, please sign!" At four o'clock in the morning, O'Doul, who evidently was having the same trouble, phoned my room.

"Do you have any kids over there?" he hollered.
"Yeah," I shouted. "Do you want some?"[28]

⌒

Upon his retirement in December 1951:

I knew I was beginning to slip as far back as three years
ago. The old timing was beginning to leave me and my
reflexes were beginning to slow up. I began to think
seriously of retiring last spring. By the end of the season
I had made up my mind definitely. It had become a
chore for me to play. I found it difficult getting out of
bed in the morning, especially after a night game. I was
full of aches and pains.

Right now I feel wonderful. But I can not forget
those torturous days and nights of agony. No, I've played
my last days of ball and I have no regrets. I feel that I
have reached the stage where I can no longer produce
for my club, my manager, my teammates, and my fans.

I had a poor year in 1951. But even if I had batted
.350, this would have been the last year for me. When
baseball is no longer fun, it's no longer a game.[29]

⌒

*On walking away from his then-baseball-record $100,000-
a-year salary:*

I would have played for nothing. I'd let the checks accumulate three or four months until I'd get a call from the general manager saying, "Cash your checks so we can make up our books."

I wanted to be a player and strictly a player. I loved the competition. I wanted to play at full speed. It got so I couldn't recoup fast enough to be at 100 percent.

They offered me the same contract in 1952 (one hundred thousand dollars) to play only seventy-five games. Can you see me playing only seventy-five games? It was a competitive thing, and it was a tough decision. It took years to build up to one hundred thousand dollars.[30]

On night baseball:

I figure night baseball cut about two years off my active career. It's tough coming back the next afternoon after playing under the lights. Night ball should be played every night, or not at all.[31]

On his desire to shine, or at least not embarrass himself, while playing in a charity ball game in Hollywood in March 1952, three months after his retirement:

I would have given anything to have hit one out of the park. But I guess those things only happen in storybooks.

It sure felt strange to swing a bat again. I followed the ball pretty good. Lindell (ex-teammate Johnny) fooled me with a curve ball on the second pitch, the rascal. It could've been worse. I could have struck out. I'm sure glad I didn't.

I know the fans were pulling for me to hit one out of the park, but it just wasn't in the cards. I sure would have liked to oblige them, though.

I wouldn't say that this is definitely the last time I ever will put on a uniform. I didn't mind going out there for a couple of minutes like I did. As a matter of fact, it was a lot of fun.[32]

On the toughest pitchers he faced:

Mel Harder of Cleveland; Bob Lemon, Cleveland; Dizzy Trout of Detroit; Art Houtteman, Detroit; and Ellis Kinder of the Red Sox.

There were many others who were tough and they seemed to get tougher for me as the years went by. But those five fellows caused me the most trouble. I can't explain it. They all had a lot of stuff. They just had my number, I guess.

Bob Feller was never as rough for me as he was to some of the others. The same of Hal Newhouser and Ned Garver. These fellows, I could hit all right. But the others—ugh![33]

On the greatest hitter he saw:

As a hitter? Ted Williams.[34]

~

On the greatest fielder he saw:

I saw my brother Dominic quite a bit. He gave me plenty of trouble. I was battling Hank Greenberg for the RBI championship one year and he took two potential triples off me, both with the bases loaded.

I said when I passed him, "You little heel." That night he came to my house for dinner. I said, "You have a hell of a nerve coming here for dinner after what you did to me." Dominic said, "Joe, I couldn't go another inch for those balls." That was his consolation to me.[35]

~

On the greatest all-around player he saw:

Charlie Gehringer of the Tigers was nearing the end of his career when I broke in, but he was the most complete ballplayer I ever saw. He could run, throw, field, and think. He was a tough clutch hitter. The best all-around.[36]

On the greatest team:

I guess the best baseball team I ever played with, or saw, was the 1937 Yankees. That was the best year I ever had, because every ball I hit seemed to be right on the nose. Even when I flied out, it would be 430 feet away. I batted .345 and I think I knocked in something like 135 or 145 runs.

On that team we had Lou Gehrig at first, Tony Lazzeri, second, Frankie Crosetti, shortstop, and Red Rolfe at third. In the outfield with me were Roy Johnson and George Selkirk. The catcher was Bill Dickey. And the pitchers included Gomez, Bump Hadley, Monte Pearson, Red Ruffing, and of course, fireman Johnny Murphy.[37]

On his greatest catch:

I guess the one I made against Hank Greenberg in the Yankee Stadium back in 1937 or '38. I caught the ball just in front of the flag pole 461 feet away from home plate. I never thought I'd get to it. I was chasing it down hoping to hold it to a triple. I stuck my glove up blind and darned if the ball didn't fall in.[38]

Harpo Speaks

On Joe McCarthy vs. Casey Stengel as managers:

I learned more under McCarthy than under anyone else in baseball. They were two different types. Stengel has revolutionized the game with his platoons. McCarthy struck on a lineup and stuck with it. I guess you'd have to say I liked McCarthy best. But don't forget the game has changed. You can't sell Casey short.

But I have a soft spot in my heart for Joe. All during my hitting streak he gave me the hit sign even when the count was 3 and 0.[39]

On playing his entire career with home games at Yankee Stadium, with its spacious plain in left-center field:

If I'd had a choice, I'd have liked to play in old Ebbets Field in Brooklyn. But I'm happy with where I played. The one thing I'm most proud of was winning all those pennants with the Yankees—ten pennants and nine world championships in my thirteen years. I sacrificed all that hitting and all those stats for what we did.[40]

On the story, long hard to nail down, that the Yankees were once close to trading him to the Red Sox for Ted Williams, putting them in home parks more suited to them:

The thing is, Williams never had a great series at Yankee Stadium. He never pumped a lot of balls out of the park. And I wouldn't have had any greater home run production at Fenway Park. I was a line-drive hitter. I didn't get the ball high. My line drives rose, but the high fence at Fenway would have kept them from going over.[41]

~

On whether he was ever thrown out of a game by an umpire:

No. I always felt the umpires were trying to do a good job and I sympathized with them. If they missed one, I'd tell them, but I wouldn't make a fuss.[42]

~

On the notion of a career as a manager:

I've never had any managerial ambitions. After all, if you are a manager, then you have to be able to get along with the newspapermen, know how to handle them as far as giving out good stories, keeping 'em posted, etc. Casey Stengel is an expert at that—maybe that may be part of the reason he is such a good manager. I doubt that I could handle it.[43]

~

On spring training:

I hated it. I never needed it.[44]

~

On what baseball needs, when asked in the fall of 1961:

I'd like to see the majors follow the suggestion Hank Greenberg made a few years ago and have interleague play. It would be wonderful. It would give the fans a chance to see the stars from the other leagues. It would stimulate attendance. It would show what the other league has. And I'm sure that over the years it would come out about even. A few games each year would make it wonderful.[45]

~

On how he would fare playing modern-era baseball:

It should be the other way around. Would some of these fellows be able to play with the talent we had then? I'm only saying that because you have twenty-six teams today. You only had sixteen teams during our time.

Also, most athletes in college used to like to get into baseball. Now all of these other sports—basketball, football—are grabbing their share. We've lost an awful lot.

The minor-league system is bad. They have so few minor leagues compared to what we had. You would spend three, four, five years down there. Now they have three ballplayers I bet don't have a total of ten games in the minor leagues and they're playing major-league ball.

Mantle came up from D ball, then B and on up. You had to have a real special skill to come up at that time. Now that it has weakened, some guys come up without going through the minor leagues.[46]

~

On why he stopped playing in Old Timers Games once he reached his sixties:

I don't want to get out there and embarrass myself. I had a lot of injuries when I played, aches and pains that are still around. My back kills me most of the time. I had operations on both my heels for bone spurs. I have arthritis and tendonitis.

If I took a cut at a ball, it would be a swing like an old woman. I don't want people to remember me that way. Right now, I couldn't throw a baseball from here to that table over there, unless I threw it underhand.[47]

~

To Ken Keltner, when he spotted him in Toronto in 1991, fifty years after the Indians third baseman helped end DiMaggio's famous streak:

Hiya, culprit.

On his status as one of the greatest American heroes of the twentieth century:

Not bad for a fellow born in Fisherman's Wharf, thinking perhaps my work was cut out to be a fisherman. At least my father thought so.[48]

DiMaggio makes his retirement official in April 1952 during a Yankee Stadium ceremony in which he turned over his No. 5 jersey to the Baseball Hall of Fame, here represented by R. D. Spraker. (AP/Wide World Photos)

THE LEGEND

"Are you the Joe DiMaggio?"
—PRINCE PHILIP, coming across Joe D.
in San Francisco in 1983

Joe DiMaggio was more than a sports hero, bigger than a star, better than a celebrity. The reach of his fame and impact can be seen in the people he befriended, the people he scorned, the people who swooned over him, the person he married.

DiMaggio went to boxing matches and sat between Dietrich and Hemingway, and two seats away was Sinatra. DiMaggio went to a gala dinner and was scheduled to sit next to Kissinger. When plans changed and DiMaggio was invited to dine with President Clinton instead, he declined. It was nothing new. When DiMaggio visited Baltimore to watch Cal Ripken Jr. break Lou Gehrig's famous streak, a Clinton emissary asked if DiMaggio would like to sit next to the president.

No.

Perhaps, the emissary went on, the president could come over and shake Joe DiMaggio's hand.

No.

And there would be no explanation. Joe DiMaggio was bigger than explanations.

When Marilyn died, he ran the funeral and shut out her Hollywood pals. He was bigger than the Rat Pack. He sent flowers to her grave for twenty years, then stopped, again without explanation.

"Joe DiMaggio has a song," marveled Derek Jeter, the Yankees shortstop and current Prince of New York. "That brings it to another level."

DiMaggio had several songs: the Les Brown ditty about the famous Streak, the Rodgers and Hammerstein tune that noted Bloody Mary's skin was "softer than DiMaggio's glove," the Simon and Garfunkel hit about Mrs. Robinson. DiMaggio wasn't hip enough to know what Simon meant by "Where have you gone, Joe DiMaggio?" but that didn't matter. A lot of solid people were confused by those times, including many legends. Sinatra ran around in Nehru jackets for a while.

DiMaggio was big. He stopped playing baseball in 1951, then spent nearly fifty years just being Joe DiMaggio. Apparently, that was enough to carry him through the century.

In 1969, he was voted the Greatest Living Ballplayer, and he was glad for the title. He insisted on being introduced as that at Old Timers Day and similar gatherings, and he insisted he be introduced last. The best for last.

Long after his last base hit, he was enticing people to patronize the Bowery Bank and to start their days with Mr. Coffee.

One day in New York, he went to a courthouse to keep a luncheon date with his friend, famed criminal lawyer Edward Bennett Williams. DiMaggio entered the courtroom during the trial, shook Williams's hand, then shook the hand of the defendant. The prosecutor jumped to his feet and objected. The judge asked what he objected to. The prosecutor said he was objecting to Joe DiMaggio.[1]

In the late eighties, he was approached to write an autobiography. He turned down $2 million to do it. By the late nineties, he could have gotten $5 million for it.[2]

People not easily impressed were impressed with him. Stephen Jay Gould, distinguished Harvard anthropologist, was fascinated by Joe DiMaggio. So was Harvard professor and Nobel physicist Edward Mills Purcell.

He went to dinner with Woody Allen and his wife, Soon-Yi, and talked movies.

Hemingway put him in the book that won him a Nobel, *The Old Man and the Sea*. Kissinger gets gooey thinking of how, just weeks after his arrival from Germany as a young teen in 1938, he visited Yankee Stadium and saw DiMaggio play.

The last two sentences legendary sportswriter Red Smith ever typed were, "I told myself not to worry. Some day there would be another Joe DiMaggio."

Lillian Gish was a silent-movie star during World War I, and during her golden years she found herself living in the same hotel as DiMaggio. She knew nothing of baseball, but she knew all about him. She and her sister secured an autographed baseball to take on a trip to Europe, placed the ball in a window in Madrid, and watched a crowd gather to gawk at it.

At a state dinner in 1987, DiMaggio produced a baseball and requested that it be signed by President Ronald Reagan and Soviet top dog Mikhail Gorbachev. Reagan took care of it the next day.

In the late 1990s, the current Yankees, who were building their own version of a dynasty, were impressed by him. Major-league ballplayers are rarely impressed by anybody. They are not automatically impressed by their distinguished predecessors—visit a big-league clubhouse on Old Timers Day, and you could hear them grumble about all the grayheads cluttering up the locker room.

The current Yankees were afraid to talk to him. Jeter, Darryl Strawberry, and David Cone admitted they were too scared to ask him for an autograph. Cone purchased a dozen balls signed by DiMaggio, instead of asking.[3]

Shortly after his death, a ball with his autograph on it was worth four hundred dollars. Some bats signed by him were worth thirty-five hundred dollars.

Among those attending his memorial service at Saint Patrick's Cathedral were Kissinger, E. L. Doctorow, Tim Russert, Bryant Gumbel, and Richard Reeves, none of them noted for indiscriminate hero worship.[4]

Nearly a year after his death, his signature on the cover of the first *Playboy* magazine—which featured

Marilyn Monroe—was auctioned for $40,250. At the same auction, Ty Cobb's dentures only brought $7,475.[5]

‿

*Film critic **Jeffrey Lyons** remembers a night in 1950, when he was five years old:*

My parents gave a party for Ethel Barrymore, and at my parents' house were Edward G. Robinson, Hemingway, Dietrich, Judy Garland and Fred Astaire, and Joe DiMaggio. I was five. I walked up to him and said, "Mr. DiMaggio, you're the best guest here."

I didn't see him for thirty-five years. He saw me at Shea Stadium and he called me over. He said, "Do you remember that night?" I said, "Vaguely." He said, "Would you still say the same thing today?"[5]

‿

Telephone Lyons's home, and the voice on the answering machine asking that you leave a message is Joe DiMaggio's.
Lyons:

That was in 1975, at an Old Timers Game. I have three hundred movie stars who have done my answering machine. From Jack Lemmon to Bette Davis, to Richard Burton to Bob Hope, to Muhammad Ali to Jack Nicholson. But I keep Joe on. Because he's Joe D. I'm a Red Sox fan, but he's above all partisanship.

I Remember Joe DiMaggio

~

Former big leaguer **Chuck Stevens** *remembers DiMaggio on the 1951 baseball tour of Japan:*

When we landed at the airport, they arranged a parade down the streets of Tokyo. We were in convertibles. There were so many people watching this parade, that Lefty O'Doul and DiMaggio, who were in the same car, called the parade off because they were afraid some of the cars might get turned over.

It was like he was a national hero. There was no contest. Joe was the man.

A Japanese fellow came to me and he was a shirt maker. He had silk. He would make 'em and they were cheap. I happened to mention it to him. He said he was interested. I said, "Let's go downtown and see what's going on." So Joe and I got in a cab and we went down to the shirt maker and we ordered shirts. We were the only two there.

This is on the Ginza, which is the Broadway of Tokyo. We leave the shirt maker's shop and now we're gonna walk down to a department store. We were just walking along chatting. And you could hear a rumble. I look back and there must have been three thousand Japanese following us. You could hear them say, "DiMaggio . . . DiMaggio."

We get to a stoplight and we're standing on a curb. And Joe's standing there, trying to act nonchalant with all these people following him. And I told him, "Man, I get so sick of this. I can't go anyplace." He whacked me on the arm and I stepped down off the curb and a cab made a right turn and only missed me by a foot or two. I said, "Jesus, Big D., you almost got me killed." He thought that was funny. He got hysterical.

Mel Parnell was also on the 1951 Japan trip:

Joe was just like a king over there. Baseball was really getting big at that time in Japan. He and Lefty O'Doul were the real big guys. Lefty, I think he could have run for Emperor over there. The Japanese were treating us royally, mainly because of these guys.

The reception was just fantastic. I remember we went on a whitewater rafting trip and Joe was pretty much sitting to the front of the boat and he got all wet. It was a little scary. Joe said he didn't care to go on one of those again.

We were the first group to go over since Babe Ruth. It was reported that the turnout to greet us was greater than MacArthur's. We were riding in cars that didn't have automatic transmissions, and they were burning up clutches because of the crowds and they couldn't hardly move.

I Remember Joe DiMaggio

Veteran Boston Herald *columnist* **George Kimball**, *not one to be impressed by celebrity, could not resist dropping Joe DiMaggio's name after a unique encounter:*

One year, the Super Bowl was in L.A. You occasionally run into this at the Super Bowl golf tournament, that you'll have really cold weather, but this was the only time I can remember bad weather in California. We played this golf tournament, and for California, it was really a cold day, in the forties and windy. I think we played only nine holes. My wife came back to join us at the dinner. She said, "How did you ever get warm?" I told her I got into the Jacuzzi. She said, "But you didn't have a bathing suit with you. You got into the hot tub naked?" I said, "Not only was I in the hot tub naked, I was in the hot tub naked with Joe DiMaggio. And he was naked, too."

Former Boston Patriots football star **Gino Cappelletti**:

I grew up in Keewatin, the iron mining country of northern Minnesota. The rest of the state was pretty much Scandinavians, but the mining country was a melting pot of nationalities, and I remember so well how important Joe DiMaggio was to us. Whenever someone with an Italian name did something noteworthy, it made us ooze with pride, gave us something to boast about.

It was at a golf tournament in California. I was putting on my shoes and when I looked over I almost gagged: "Oh, my God, Joe DiMaggio!" I was no kid, but I felt just like a kid again when I introduced myself and asked if I could have an autograph for my Uncle Vic, who absolutely loved the man. Joe said sure, and he was just as gracious as I'd always imagined he'd be.[6]

Dario Lodigiani remembers DiMaggio's star power, even in the middle of a world war:

We played over there in Honolulu Stadium. They packed that ballpark. All the GIs were at the ball game all the time.

We lived in a big Quonset hut over on the field. Joe was with us. He played cards with the guys. He'd sit around and talk to the guys. Everybody knew Joe DiMaggio was stationed at Hickam Field. Some of the officers would come in and invite him here or there. They'd introduce him to some of the big wheels.

Charlie Silvera:

We were consigned to barracks, up waiting to get a ship to go over, and when they found out we were there, they made us play a ball game. We ended up getting leave, a pass to go out at night. Before that, we were restricted. But because of Joe, we had liberty every night. That was one of Joe's deals.

Another deal was, he had a couple of cases of scotch that he had brought with him. When we packed our barracks bags to go on the ship, he couldn't carry it all, so Joe dispersed it to different people. I don't think he got his two cases back at the end.

He wanted his private life to remain private, and he hated to be on display, but that didn't matter. After a few years with the Yankees, DiMaggio was public property.

He married minor movie actress Dorothy Arnold in 1939, and it was called the biggest gala wedding ever in San Francisco. Fans climbed trees and stood on rooftops to get a glimpse of the couple leaving the church.

Dino Restelli *was one of them:*

They got married at the Saints Peter and Paul church in San Francisco, in North Beach. They were repairing the church at the time. They had a big scaffolding in the front of the church. They were putting on big sheets of material to finish the church, because the church was repaired piecemeal.

This buddy of mine and I, we jumped on the scaffolding and we laid on the scaffolding looking into the church. We saw the procession come into the church, go all the way up to the altar. They left the door open because there were thousands of people outside, waiting for them to come out. When we watched them coming out, we kind of moved and some of the dust came down through the scaffolding and Joe kind of looked up and laughed. He saw the two of us up there.

⁓

Bobby Brown remembers the newlywed DiMaggio in Japan in 1954:

I had gone to Korea with the Forty-fifth Division. After serving over there for about a year, I rotated to Japan. So when Joe and Marilyn came to Japan, I was stationed at the Tokyo army hospital.

In Japan, it was worse. They had five or six million people lining the streets waiting to see him, when he and Marilyn flew in from the airport. They were four or five deep all the way from the airport to Tokyo.

Joe and Marilyn were on their honeymoon. Joe was going to help Lefty O'Doul, the manager of the Seals, conduct some clinics with the Japanese major-league teams.

I got temporary duty to go on that tour with Joe and Lefty O'Doul, and we had our wives with us. We were all together. To me, he was Joe, and she (Monroe) was a real nice gal. We had a great time together. We would give those clinics, and the Japanese would entertain us at night. Now Marilyn, after a few days, went over to

Korea and spent some time with the troops. And then she came on back.

The Japanese just went wild. At that time, the two biggest things in the Japanese' lives were baseball players and movie stars, and you had the two biggest, right there.

⁓

DiMaggio became a folk hero with Marilyn, and folk heroes spawn tall stories. One of them that has lasted over the decades is that Chicago White Sox catcher **Gus Zernial** *was responsible for Joe and Marilyn getting together.*

Zernial recalls that tale was a product of the myth-making machine:

Back in the early fifties, I don't know exactly what year it was, Marilyn was at Pasadena when I was there training with the White Sox. Spring training. We had quite a photo shoot. We had other guys involved. Eddie Robinson was there, Hank Majeski, myself. I took a lot of pictures with her. It was just a photo-op for her, more than anything. She was a young starlet at the time. It was nothing more than just posing together. Bats and balls were involved. Teaching her how to hit a baseball. Stuff like that. It was nothing more than that. That was the story. She was absolutely super. She was one of the brightest young people you would ever want to talk to. I might add to that, I was so disappointed in the movies they put her in after that. They depicted her as a dumb blonde. She certainly wasn't that. She was a very lovely lady and a very bright young lady.

A lot of pictures came out at that particular time. They were distributed everywhere. *Esquire* magazine carried a lot of them. That was all there was to it. That was the only time I ever met her.

Joe never really talked to me about it. He saw the pictures and made the comment to some of the writers in New York (that he'd like to meet Marilyn). The story's been twisted over the years. I'll tell you the exact story.

We went to New York. Of course, Joe was in center field. And Marilyn was in New York at the same time. She was doing her thing. I had no idea that she was even in New York. But Joe had found out that she was in New York, and he managed to get an introduction to her. Somehow or another, the writers got me involved in it as directly introducing Marilyn to Joe. That didn't happen. It was a coincidental thing that we were in New York at the same time. Had I had the opportunity to introduce her, I probably would have done so. I didn't have that opportunity. But he got the introduction. And from there on, they got together.

The story was twisted over the years. Joe didn't have some nice things to say about me, because he thought I was trying to take credit, trying to take some glory road for introducing her. Which didn't happen.

I admired Joe as a ballplayer and I admired Marilyn Monroe as an individual. They're truly two legends, and somehow or another, I got caught in between. I just happen to know both those people. And it's good memories for me.

~

DiMaggio doubled his celebrity status when he married Monroe. The ceremony lasted five minutes, the marriage lasted 274 days. The fascination lasted forever. DiMaggio had managed to live out two of the top American male daydreams of the twentieth century: He played center field for the Yankees, and he married Marilyn Monroe.

Jimmy Cannon called them "folk idols. The whole country's pets." Even after they were divorced, they were a hot item. Imagine Michael Jordan coupled with Princess Diana.

*Longtime newspaperman **Eddie Corsetti**, then working for the* Boston American, *remembers a DiMaggio-Monroe stakeout in January 1955:*

He was at Dom's house in Wellesley with Marilyn Monroe. We were all waiting for the guy to come out. Not him necessarily, but for him and Marilyn. There were a lot of us waiting. You had something like eleven newspapers in Boston at the time.

Carroll Myett was the photographer with me. We were in my car. A brand-new spanking Ford. Black and white. It looked like a police car. We're sitting there waiting for two or three hours. It looked as though something was going to happen. But I didn't think that Joe was going to have a press conference.

So we got in my car, Carroll and I, and we drove off around the corner. Sure enough, Joe comes out with Marilyn Monroe and gets into a Cadillac convertible and drove off. And we followed them. She was wearing a big floppy hat and sunglasses. Carroll was the one who spotted them.

I don't know how many towns we went through. But he must have driven five miles before he realized I was behind him. We were on Route 9 headed west. I don't know where he was going. Maybe he was going back to New York.

Carroll had his camera, one of the big old cameras, up by the windshield. I don't know if DiMaggio, looking through the rearview mirror, saw this car following him with this guy with a camera. But he put on the gas. And I mean he took off.

We're following him and he had to be going eighty miles an hour. Carroll keeps saying, "You're going to get us killed." I'm hoping like hell the state troopers would show up and stop him. I'm trying to pull alongside of him so Carroll can get a shot. As I try to pull alongside him, he pulls his car to the left. I have to brake and back down.

We must have chased him for fifteen to twenty miles. He put it in overdrive. He had to be going a hundred miles per hour. I said, "This is crazy. I'm driving this Ford, and he's driving a Cadillac." We let him go.

I'll give him credit. He was a helluva driver.

They were as big as anything in the country at the time.

Two Yankee legends were on the same roster in 1951, with DiMaggio about to retire and Mickey Mantle breaking in as a rookie fresh out of Oklahoma. (AP/Wide World Photos)

New York saloonkeeper **Toots Shor**:

I remember one time little Frankie Graham from the
Journal was in the joint. He had an appointment to
interview Alex Webster. He was the running star of the
Giants then, and DiMaggio happened to be in the
place. Graham came in and Alex was sitting at a table
over on the side, and he kept looking at DiMaggio.
Finally, Graham asked Webster who he was looking at.
Webster said he was looking at DiMaggio and he had
always been his hero, and he asked Frankie if he knew
him. So Frankie took him over to meet Joe. His eyes
were popping out of his head. Alex was the biggest football player in New York then, but when he was introduced to Joe, he was like a little kid.[7]

Jerry Coleman *remembers DiMaggio's star power in
another war:*

I went to Vietnam with this guy in 1967. With Pete
Rose, Tony Conigliaro, myself, and DiMaggio. You've
got Rose and Conigliaro, the hotshots of that era, and
wherever we went, they didn't want to see us. They
wanted to see DiMaggio. I don't care what the age was,
whether they were nineteen or forty-five, the generals
down to the buck privates, it was DiMaggio everybody
wanted to see. This man never lost the tremendous aura
that he had.

201

I Remember Joe DiMaggio

John McNamara was a rookie coach with DiMaggio with the 1968 Oakland Athletics:

One of the biggest thrills I've ever had in my life was when we went to New York. We had a day game. He called me up in my room and said, "Meet me in the lobby and we'll get a ride to the ballpark." We had to walk about five blocks to get to this photographer's car and he drove us to Yankee Stadium.

Joe actually stopped traffic. Taxicabs and garbage trucks and delivery trucks and anything you can imagine. They stopped. They were honking their horns. He's waving to them.

Then to go to Yankee Stadium for the first time as a participant and to walk into that ballpark with him is something that was very, very special to me. I'll never forget it. We got to the bottom of the stairs and he said, "Which way do we turn?" I said, "I don't know. I've never been down here. Which way did you turn as a Yankee?" He said, "To the right." I said, "Well, I think we ought to go to the left."

Sal Bando was a young infielder on the 1968 Athletics:

He was the most recognized person I've ever been around. We'd come into airports and it didn't matter what time it was, people would stop and point at him. And that was before he did the Mr. Coffee commercials. It was the way he carried himself. He retired at the peak of his career, he was married to Marilyn Monroe, he was always a gentleman, he never used foul language. He was the complete package.[8]

University of New Hampshire professor of kinesiology **Ron Croce** *was playing professional baseball in Italy when he met Joe DiMaggio:*

It must have been around 1972. When I was playing ball over in Italy, he came over and was making his grand tour. He came to our practice. I had a coffee with him and a brioche, or something like that. This was in Florence.

There was a rumor that he was showing up, and we thought the Italians were pulling our legs. He actually showed up, he interacted with us, talked with us a little bit about how baseball was, about how we were enjoying ourselves.

This is this icon. I heard my dad talk about him I don't know how many times. You know, "No one played center field like Joe D.; he never made a mistake running the bases; fifty-six-game hitting streak, and after it stopped he had another sixteen-game hitting streak." I never saw him play. It was quite an experience. He seemed like an extremely nice man. You hear all these things about him now. But that's not what we encountered. He just seemed like a helluva nice man. Distinguished, dressed in a suit.

All the ballplayers knew of Joe D. as one of the great ballplayers of all time. When baseball started to really get going in Italy in the late forties, early fifties, I think he might have made some tours in Italy.

A lot of them also knew about Marilyn Monroe. The joke was they were going to ask him about Marilyn Monroe. I said, "No, no, no, don't ask him about that."

He was well known, even in Italy. The people who follow baseball in Italy, which is fairly large, knew of Joe DiMaggio. They said, "Wow." Almost like we did.

Sparky Anderson was manager of the Big Red Machine version of the Cincinnati Reds when he met DiMaggio at a dinner in 1972:

Someone introduced me to him and I said, "Mr. DiMaggio, I'm very nervous." He said, "Why?" I said, "Because since I was a young man, I've heard about you and thought about you, and you were baseball to me. Just being in your presence makes me nervous." He said, "You are very kind."[9]

THE LEGEND

Future Hall of Famer **Al Kaline** *met Joe DiMaggio in 1951:*

I was still in high school. I went to New York to play in the Hearst All-Star game. They took us through the locker room, and Joe was sitting in front of his locker. I stopped and shook his hand. It was like meeting a god.

~

Ed Lynch *pitched for the New York Mets and for the Chicago Cubs and served as a baseball executive in several positions, including general manager of the Cubs.*

He was born five years after DiMaggio retired, but became smitten with the legend like many late-born baby boomers:

I grew up in the New York area. I was a big Yankee fan. A big, big Yankee fan. Mickey Mantle was like God. I'm forty-four years old—when I was a kid, Mickey was coming to the end of his career, but he was a legend in New York at that time. In 1968, when that Simon and Garfunkel song came out—"Where have you gone, Joe DiMaggio?"—for some reason that sort of sparked my interest. I started reading about him. My dad grew up in New York, was a Yankee fan, and he knew about Joe DiMaggio. He talked to me about how big he was in New York and how he epitomized the Yankees. The Yankee Clipper and those championship years. So I just started reading everything I could get my hands on.

I Remember Joe DiMaggio

When I was a kid, I saw him at an Old Timers Game at Yankee Stadium. I think it was about '67. He was introduced—he was introduced last, of course. That was before they refurbished the stadium. It was like basically the same stadium he played in. You looked around and you could see Death Valley—460 feet to deep left center—and the flagpole and the monuments out there and the facade going all the way around. Just seeing him out on that field, you're thinking, *Geez, it could be 1941 again*. It really did bring you back to an era when the Yankees were the club, and he was the Yankee Clipper. He was the guy.

We moved to Miami in 1968. My dad went to work for Eastern Air Lines, so we would get to fly around to various sporting events. We went to the 1969 All-Star Game in Washington, D.C. We were staying at the hotel, which was the headquarters. They had a banquet where they named the greatest player, the greatest living player. This is going to sound like a corny story, but it was in the grand ballroom at this hotel. I snuck in and was up on the balcony, with the lights and everything, and watched that dinner. When he got named the Greatest Living Player, that was really a thrill. It was the year after I had just starting reading about him. To see him in person and to see his greatness brought to the present time as the Greatest Living Player—I mean, you had guys up there like Willie Mays, Ted Williams, Bob Gibson, some great, great players—to be named the Greatest Living Player was a hell of an achievement.

In 1992, I was the minor-league director for the San Diego Padres. We hosted the All-Star Game that year. On the day before the game, when they have the batting practices and the open workout, I was sitting with Joe McIlvaine in his box at Jack Murphy Stadium. Our director of promotions came in and said, "Listen, I've got this celebrity that I kind of made this mistake on his tickets. They put him out in the stands. Do you guys mind if he sits in here with you?" And we're thinking, *Oh, great. It's going to be like a talk-show host or something.* We said, "Well, who is it?" They said, "Joe DiMaggio." We almost fell off our chairs. We said, "Of course."

I got to sit with Joe for about two and a half hours, right next to him, and watch the workout. He had (memorabilia czar) Barry Halper and a couple of other guys with him.

Joe was just talking about baseball in general. I knew a lot about his career, reading everything about his career. I started asking him some questions. I didn't want to be too pushy. I asked him why he thought he hit the ball so well in Fenway Park. He said he saw the ball well there. I asked him about when he was a rookie and his foot was burned by the trainer. We talked about that some. He didn't make his debut until about three weeks after the season started his rookie year.

One interesting thing Joe McIlvaine asked him, "Do you ever go out to games very often? Just sit in the stands?" And Joe pointed out at the fans and said, "I'd like to. But they won't let me." He was pointing out at the fans. They won't leave him alone. I think that really told a story about celebrity and the limitations on his freedom to move about. I thought that was kind of sad.

I REMEMBER JOE DIMAGGIO

After about an hour and a half, Barry Halper was there with Joe. There was a break and I ran down to my office and I got one of those commemorative All-Star balls that we were using, with the colored seams. I came back up and I said to Barry, "Barry, do you think Joe would sign a ball for me?" Was I nervous? Yes and no. Yes, because his reputation preceded him. And no, because he was sitting in our area. We were very nice to him. I thought it wasn't an unreasonable request. Barry said he wasn't sure, that he was very touchy about this kind of thing. He said, "Let me ask him for you."

So he went over and whispered something to Joe and Joe turned around and gave me a look. Oh, geez, you know? Then he said, "Is this ball for you?" I said, "Yes sir, it is." So he wrote on there, "To Ed Lynch, Best Wishes, Joe DiMaggio." If I can find a guy named Ed Lynch with a lot of money, I could probably do pretty well. But seriously, it's one of my most prized possessions. I've got it locked up in my office here in my home.

He started talking about why he was upset regarding autographs, the forgeries and everything. I'll tell you, after listening to him, I could understand. He just said that over the years he's just seen hundreds and hundreds of bogus autographs. He had a little thing he did. He put a couple of dots in the last "O" in DiMaggio, as his little thing, so he could tell what was a real signature or not. I'm sure somebody noticed that and starting copying it. He said he did little things to his signature to make it look unique so he would know that he had signed it. Just think about it. I mean, I'm walking in the mall and I see a Joe DiMaggio ball in one of these collector's stores for $850. I'm sure over the years a lot of people made a lot of money off of forgeries. That would upset me, too, if it was my name and I felt like I was being exploited like that.

At that time he was seventy-eight years old. I remember looking at him when he was walking out. He had slowed down, obviously. But he had big hands. You could tell at one time that he was a big, strong guy. I was very impressed with him.

Bernie Esser remembers twenty-four hours with DiMaggio, illustrative of the life of a Living Legend:

You know the Old Timers Games, the Crackerjack games? They played in Washington, then moved them up to Buffalo. Joe always made it to those things. He had a gofer when he was in the East. And we were up in Buffalo and they were having this cocktail party the night before, and Joe comes in and there's no gofer. He's all by himself. As soon as he comes into something, people get around him. I had been sitting with Bob Feller and his wife. They had a little table against the wall. So I said, "Joe, come over here and sit down with them and I'll go get you something to eat."

When I came back, I could hardly get to him because the people are asking him for an autograph. I politely said, "Can I get in here? I know Joe will sign after he eats. Give the man a break." So he had something to eat and he said, "Okay." And I kind of lined people up so it wasn't a total mess. Halfway through, one lady spills a drink on him. He brushes it off. Everybody that wanted an autograph got an autograph in the hour, hour and a half that he was there. He had to go do some TV thing and I went to bed. My reason for being there is I had a ton of books and I would be down in the lobby getting my books autographed. That's why I went there. I did very, very well. I'm just about to go downstairs and the phone rings and it was Joe. And he said, "Have you eaten?" I said no. He said, "Come down to the players thing and we'll have breakfast." So I did. And when we were in there, he was the only person in there, and I swear every maid in the place came down while we were sitting there and were getting his autograph. They had a guard outside so only hotel people could get to him.

They had a limo for him. And the guy comes and says, "What would you like to do today, Joe?" And he says, "I'd like to go up to Niagara Falls. Bernie, will you come with me?" I didn't want to. I wanted to be down in the lobby. But I said, "Sure, I'll go with you." So we got up to Niagara Falls.

We get up there and we're not there more than ten minutes until somebody recognizes Joe DiMaggio. And here we go. The stupid autograph business again. We leave. He wanted a bowl of minestrone soup. So this fella took us to some restaurant in a residential area. It had this one Italian restaurant. And when we walked in the place, there were maybe two people in the bar and two people in the restaurant. In the next half-hour, the place half filled up. The owner was calling his friends in the neighborhood and people were coming down to get autographs. We finished the soup and he does his thing with them, and as we're walking out to get in the car, a guy is running down the street. "Joe! Joe!" He had a ball. He got the autograph.

So we go back to the hotel. Before he goes upstairs, he says, "I want you to go out to the ballpark with me. I'll meet you at five." All the other ballplayers left at four o'clock. But not one person left that lobby, because they knew DiMaggio was still in the house and they wanted to get his autograph.

The driver came down and said, "Joe doesn't want to go through this anymore right now. We're going to go down the back elevator." We did that. As we're getting into the car, somebody spots us and they circled the car and he signs a few and he says, "I've got to get out to the ballpark." Off we go.

You could drive into the new Buffalo ballpark with an automobile, behind the stands where all the concessionaires were and so forth. We drive in there and Joe says, "Where's the clubhouse?" The driver said, "It's down there about fifty yards or so." Joe said, "Well, let me out here." The driver said, "Joe, all the concession people will be on you." He said, "That's all right. They're my fans." So he walked slowly and he signed autographs. And now we go into the clubhouse. And I've just about had autographs up to my ears. And I'm not even the guy who's signing them. In fact I thought, *I'll never ask anybody for another autograph again.* But anyway, we go into the clubhouse. And I'm thinking, *Now. Now, he's okay.*

He didn't even get to sit down and Enos Slaughter has a dozen balls for him to sign. So it's no better in there with all the players than anywhere else he had been.

They gave him a pair of baseball shoes. He said to me, "Do you want a pair of baseball shoes?" And I said, "Yeah, sure." I don't know why. I have absolutely no use for them. So they give me a pair of shoes.

I go out and I was wandering around, enjoying myself. And Joe is sitting in there, signing. He decides he's going to go up and watch an inning from some box. He said, "When you get back to the hotel, call me." There was going to be a cocktail party after the ball game. So I did. He said, "Okay, come on up." I thought, *What does he want me to come up there for? What does he have?* He has my free shoes for me. He carried them all the way back from the stadium. He didn't bring his own, but he brought mine. I got my shoes and we go down to the after-game party and it's the same routine. People asking him for his autograph. And he signed. At about ten o'clock, he said, "I'm going up to go to bed. I'm leaving early in the morning." I said, "Thanks for a wonderful day, Joe." And it was. I'll remember that forever. It was just a marvelous day.

THE LEGEND

Toronto Blue Jays pitcher **David Wells** *met Joe DiMaggio in 1997:*

Anybody who has grown up a fan of baseball, especially a Yankee fan, and you get to sit there and talk with one of their legends just gives you goose bumps. A lot of people had a difficult time getting autographs from him, but when I walked in there he said, "Sure, Dave, what do you want signed?"

Like, wow, that's awesome.

Notes

Chapter 1

1. Maury Allen, *Where Have You Gone, Joe DiMaggio?* (New York: E. P. Dutton and Co., 1975), p. 40.
2. Donald Honig, *Baseball When the Grass Was Real* (New York: Coward, McCann & Geoghegan, Inc., 1975), pp. 229–230.
3. George De Gregorio, *Joe DiMaggio—An Informal Biography* (New York: Stein and Day, 198)1, p. 249.
4. Ibid., p. 249.
5. *Boston Globe*, March 11, 1968.

Chapter 2

1. *USA Today*, March 9, 1999.
2. *New York Daily News*, April 25, 1999.
3. John Tullius, *I'd Rather Be a Yankee* (New York: Macmillan, 1986), p. 148.
4. *Boston Herald*, June 24, 1941.
5. Allen, p. 106.

Chapter 3

1. *Cincinnati Post*, March 10, 1999.
2. *New York Times*, February 8, 1979.

3. *Boston Record*, July 4, 1948.
4. Al Silverman, *Joe DiMaggio—The Golden Year 1941* (Englewood Cliffs, N.J.: Prentice-Hall, 1969), p. 249.
5. Tullius, p. 128.
6. *Boston Globe*, March 9, 1999.
7. Tullius, pp. 127–128.
8. *Denver Post*, March 9, 1999.
9. *New York Times*, April 2, 1999.
10. *Boston Globe*, June 30, 1966.
11. *Boston Herald*, September 5, 1950.
12. *Boston Herald*, December 13, 1951.
13. *Boston Herald*, November 13, 1951.

Chapter 4
1. Allen, p. 45.
2. Silverman, p. 113.
3. Ibid., p. 82.
4. *New York Times*, October 22, 2000.
5. Allen, p. 60.
6. Frank Gifford and Harry Waters, *The Whole Ten Yards* (New York: Random House, 1993), pp. 217–218.
7. *New York Times*, May 15, 1978.

Chapter 5
1. *Boston Post*, October 28, 1954.
2. *New York Times*, March 31, 1963.
3. *Boston Herald*, June 22, 1950.
4. Joe DiMaggio, *Lucky to Be a Yankee* (New York: Grossett and Dunlap, 1947), p. 105.
5. *Boston Record*, March 10, 1961.
6. *New York Times*, March 31, 1963.
7. *Boston Evening Globe*, October 5, 1954.

NOTES

8. Bill Gutman, *Giants of Baseball* (New York: Gutman, 1975).
9. *Boston Evening Globe*, April 19, 1938.
10. *Boston Herald*, October 4, 1948.
11. *Boston Sunday Advertiser*, May 6, 1962.
12. Ibid.
13. *Boston Herald*, October 4, 1948.
14. *Boston Evening Globe*, September 10, 1959.
15. *Boston Herald*, March 10, 1961.
16. *Boston Herald-American*, August 2, 1978.
17. *Boston Herald*, July 2, 1941.
18. Silverman, p. 178.
19. *Boston American*, March 5, 1942.
20. Tullius, pp. 158–159.
21. *Boston Herald*, October 4, 1948.
22. *Boston Herald*, April 15, 1949.
23. *Boston Herald*, May 18, 1986.
24. *Boston Herald*, June 22, 1952.
25. *New York Times*, March 31, 1963.
26. *Boston Herald*, December 15, 1951.
27. *Boston Herald*, July 27, 1951.
28. *Boston Herald*, June 22, 1952.
29. Associated Press, December 12, 1951.
30. *Boston Herald*, November 18, 1964.
31. *Boston Record*, December 12, 1951.
32. *Boston Herald*, March 19, 1952.
33. *Boston Herald*, February 29, 1952.
34. *Boston Herald*, January 28, 1955.
35. Ibid.
36. *Boston Traveler*, November 19, 1961.
37. Ibid.
38. Associated Press, December 12, 1951.
39. *Boston Herald*, August 31, 1958.
40. *Boston Herald*, May 18, 1986.

41. *Boston Herald*, February 10, 1985.
42. *Boston Globe*, March 11, 1968.
43. United Press, April 6, 1953.
44. *Boston American*, February 22, 1971.
45. *Boston Herald*, November 19, 1961.
46. *Boston Herald*, May 11, 1986.
47. *Boston Herald*, September 26, 1976.
48. *New York Times*, April 11, 1972.

Chapter 6

1. *Washington Post*, March 16, 1999.
2. *Boston Globe*, March 9, 1999.
3. *San Diego Union-Tribune*, March 9, 1999.
4. *New York Daily News*, April 25, 1999.
5. *Playboy*, February 1, 2000.
6. *Boston Herald*, March 10, 1999.
7. Allen, p. 97.
8. *Los Angeles Times*, March 9, 1999.
9. Ibid.

INDEX

Ali, Muhammad, 189
Allen, Soon-Yi, 187
Allen, Mel, 112
Allen, Woody, 187
Almada, Louis, 6-7, 68-70, 123-24
Anderson, Sparky, 204
Appel, Marty, 140
Appling, Luke, 35
Arnold, Dorothy, 194-95
Astaire, Fred, 189
Auerbach, Red, 19, 88
Auker, Eldon, 40
Averill, Earl, 9

Babich, Johnny, 40-41, 163
Bagby, Tim, 165
Bando, Sal, 202-03
Barath, Steve, 99-100
Barrow, Ed, 165-67
Barrymore, Ethel, 189
Bauer, Hank, 171
Berra, Yogi, 90, 140
Bevens, Bill, 63
Blount, Roy Jr., 125
Bodie, Ping, 156
Booke, Ike, 156

Bordagaray, Frenchy, 106
Bothello, Eddie, 56-57
Boudreau, Lou, 44, 48, 75-76
Breslin, Jimmy, 1
Brown, Bobby, 18, 22, 62, 71, 86-87, 110, 116, 195-96
Brown, Les, 30, 186
Burton, Richard, 189

Caime, Dick, 84
Cameron, Diane, 129-31
Cannon, Jimmy, 5, 52, 66, 114, 198
Cappelletti, Gino, 192-93
Cater, Danny, 125
Caveney, Ike, 156
Chandler, Raymond, 30
Chandler, Spud, 11
Chapman, Ben, 7
Clinton, Bill, 185-86
Cobb, Ty, 30
Coleman, Jerry, 4-6, 18-19, 26, 37-38, 52, 55, 66, 86, 87, 89-91, 110, 127, 201
Cone, David, 188
Conigliaro, Tony, 201

Cooper, Gary, 21
Corsetti, Eddie, 198-99
Corum, Bill, 114
Croce, Ron, 203-04
Cronin, Joe, 59
Crosby, Bing, 84
Crosetti, Frank, 59, 64, 85,
    107-08, 157-58, 178
Curtis, Chad, 79

Daley, Arthur, 114
Daniel, Dan, 45
Daresta, Louis, 58
Davis, Bette, 189
De la Hoya, Oscar, 137
Dickey, Bill, 17, 49, 59,
    159, 178
Dietrich, Marlene, 2, 185,
    189
DiMaggio, Dominic "Dom,"
    5, 39, 44, 57-58, 94, 99,
    104, 128, 138, 160, 177
DiMaggio, Tom, 105
DiMaggio, Vince, 45, 65, 128
Doerr, Bobby, 24, 66, 73,
    81, 91
Durso, Joe, 144

Eckhardt, Oscar, 69
Edmonds, Jimmy, 78
Effrat, Looie, 114
Engelberg, Morris, 143-46
Esser, Bernie, 139-47, 209-12
Evans, Dwight, 1

Feen, Vernon, 53-54
Feller, Bob, 35, 61
Fenton, Jode, 157
Ferriss, Boo, 20, 38-39, 86
Fitzgerald, Barry, 84
Ford, Whitey, 82, 112
Fothergill, Fat, 1
Foxx, Jimmie, 17
Furillo, Carl, 54

Galan, Augie, 67
Garland, Judy, 189
Gehrig, Lou, 92, 138, 169,
    178, 185
Gehringer, Charlie, 177
Gibson, Bob, 206
Gifford, Frank, 122-23
Gionfriddo, Al, 27-28, 128
Gish, Lillian, 187-88
Glick, Betty, 91-92
Gomez, Lefty, 49, 59, 100-
    01, 102-03, 105-06, 140,
    159, 178
Goodman, Billy, 85
Gorbachev, Mikhail, 188
Gordon, Joe, 24
Gould, Stephen J., 187
Graham, Charlie, 68-69
Graham, Frankie, 201
Greenberg, Hank, 9, 11, 97,
    101, 177, 178
Gumbel, Bryant, 188

Hadley, Bump, 178

Halper, Barry, 146, 207-08
Harder, Mel, 35, 176
Harris, Patricia Donnelly, 117-18
Harris, Robin, 117
Harris, Stephen, 133-34
Hemingway, Ernest, 21, 185, 187, 189
Henrich, Tommy, 4, 9, 17, 18, 24-26, 37, 39, 40-42, 43, 46-47, 51, 55, 61, 64, 71, 74-75, 101-02, 144
Holmes, Tommy, 11-12
Hoover, J. Edgar, 118
Hope, Bob, 189
Hornsby, Rogers, 30, 37
Houtteman, Art, 176
Hubley, Jim, 59-60
Hughes, Howard, 155
Hughson, Tex, 25

Irvin, Monte, 93

Jeter, Derek, 186, 188
Joiner, Roy, 23
Jolley, Smead, 156
Jordan, Michael, 5
Joost, Eddie, 34, 87, 90

Kaline, Al, 205
Katz, Michael, 136-37
Keeler, Wee Willie, 41, 43, 163-64
Keller, Charlie, 18, 61

Kelly, George, 140
Keltner, Ken, 44, 48, 164, 183
Kimball, George, 136-37, 192
Kinder, Ellis, 176
Kissinger, Henry, 185, 188
Kuzuru, Makoto, 173

Lang, Jack, 82-83, 135-36
Lavagetto, Cookie, 64
Lazzeri, Tony, 59, 107-08, 157-58, 159, 178
Lemmon, Jack, 189
Lemon, Bob, 176
Lincoln, Abraham, 30
Lindell, Johnny, 176
Lodigiani, Dario, 2-3, 6, 16, 31-32, 35, 36-37, 53, 66, 98-99, 111, 193
Lopat, Eddie, 63, 75-76
Luciano, Lucky, 118
Luckman, Sid, 88
Lynch, Ed, 205-09
Lyons, Doug, 118, 129
Lyons, Jeffrey, 189
Lyons, Leonard, 118, 129

Madden, Bill, 146
Mailho, Emil, 34
Majeski, Hank, 196
Manning, Rick, 78
Mantle, Mickey, 20, 93, 112, 182, 200, 205

Marlowe, Philip, 30
Martin, Billy 112, 126
Mays, Willie, 8, 13, 21, 72, 124, 206
McCarthy, Joe, 7-8, 12, 17, 19, 25, 40, 46, 62-63, 81, 103-04, 158, 179
McDougald, Gil, 76-77
McInnis, Stuffy, 1
McIlvaine, Joe, 207-08
McNamara, John, 125-26, 202
Monroe, Marilyn, 113, 116, 117-18, 154, 155, 159-60, 186, 188, 195-99, 203, 204
Murphy, Johnny, 62, 101-02, 107, 178
Myett, Carroll, 198-99

Newsom, Bobo, 32
Newsom, Buck, 32
Nicholson, Jack, 189

O'Doul, Lefty, 16, 56, 68, 94-95, 147, 156, 173, 190, 191, 195
Onisko, Danny, 119-21
Owen, Mickey, 25

Parker, Everett, 12-13, 38, 44, 118-19
Parnell, Mel, 79, 83, 85, 96, 115-16, 191

Pearson, Monte, 178
Pesky, Johnny, 66, 67
Polonia, Luis, 79
Power, Tyrone, 92
Prince Philip, 185
Purcell, Edward Mills, 187

Raimondi, Bill, 23, 70, 111
Reagan, Ronald, 188
Reeves, Richard, 188
Rego, Jimmy, 56-57, 70
Restelli, Dino, 94-95, 137-39, 194-95
Reynolds, Allie, 60
Rice, Grantland "Granny," 114
Rickey, Branch, 2
Ripken, Cal Jr., 185
Rizzuto, Phil, 1, 18, 36, 44-45, 76, 90, 93, 103-04, 112
Roberts, Robin, 60
Robinson, Bojangles, 43
Robinson, Edward G., 189, 196
Rodgers and Hammerstein, 186
Rolfe, Red, 39, 46, 59, 178
Rose, Pete, 29, 201
Rubalcava, Charlie, 124
Ruffing, Red, 59, 159, 178
Russert, Tim, 188
Ruth, Babe, 30, 57, 138, 191

INDEX

Salinger, J. D., 155
Sapio, Angelo, 31
Sales, Bob, 134
Selkirk, George, 178
Shea, Frank, 64
Sheed, Wilfred, 8
Shor, Toots, 2, 114, 117, 119
Silvera, Charlie, 34, 112-13, 145-46, 193-94
Simon and Garfunkel, 186, 205
Sinatra, Frank, 2, 185, 186
Sisler, George, 37, 42
Sisto, Ernie, 13-14
Slaughter, Enos, 22, 212
Smith, Al, 164-65
Smith, Edgar, 35
Smith, Red, 114, 187
Solotaire, George, 117, 118
Spence, Stan, 43
Spraker, R. D., 184
Stengel, Casey, 2, 77, 85, 89, 90, 91, 168, 171, 179, 180
Stevens, Chuck, 21, 22, 62, 108, 126-27, 190-91
Stine, Lee, 32, 67, 102-03
Strawberry, Darryl, 188
Sturm, Johnny, 17-18, 45-46, 72, 104-07
Suplizio, Sam, 14-15, 77-79, 133

Terry, Bill, 59
Thurston, Hollis, 156
Trosky, Hal, 15
Trout, Dizzy, 37, 176
Truman, Harry, 1

Vetrano, Joe Jr., 147-53
Vitt, Ossie, 15

Washington, George, 30
Webster, Alex, 201
Wells, David, 213
Whitaker, Pernell, 137
Whitman, Walt, 8
Williams, Edward Bennett, 187
Williams, Ted, 2, 13, 21, 30, 39, 69-70, 72, 73, 77, 85, 142, 177, 179-80, 206
Wilson, Hack, 30
Winchell, Walter, 141
Woods, Tiger, 5
Wyatt, Whitlow, 24-25

Yount, Robin, 78

Zernial, Gus, 122, 196-98
Zuber, Bill, 79

ABOUT THE AUTHOR

David Cataneo is a former award-winning reporter, baseball columnist, and editor for the *Boston Herald*. His previous books include *Peanuts and Crackerjack*, *Hornsby Hit One Over My Head*, and *Tony C*, a finalist for the 1997 Casey Award for best baseball book.